MANDALA ANIMAL ADULT COLORING BOOK

COPYRIGHT © 2022 BY STEAM MILL PRESS

All rights reserved. No part of this publication may be reproduced or used in any manner whatsoever without the express written permission of the author except for the use of brief quotations in a book review.

GET CONNECTED!

Follow Steam Mill Press for the latest news and upcoming designs.

Amazon - https://www.amazon.com/author/steammillpress

Facebook - https://www.facebook.com/steammillpress

THIS COLORING BOOK BELONGS TO

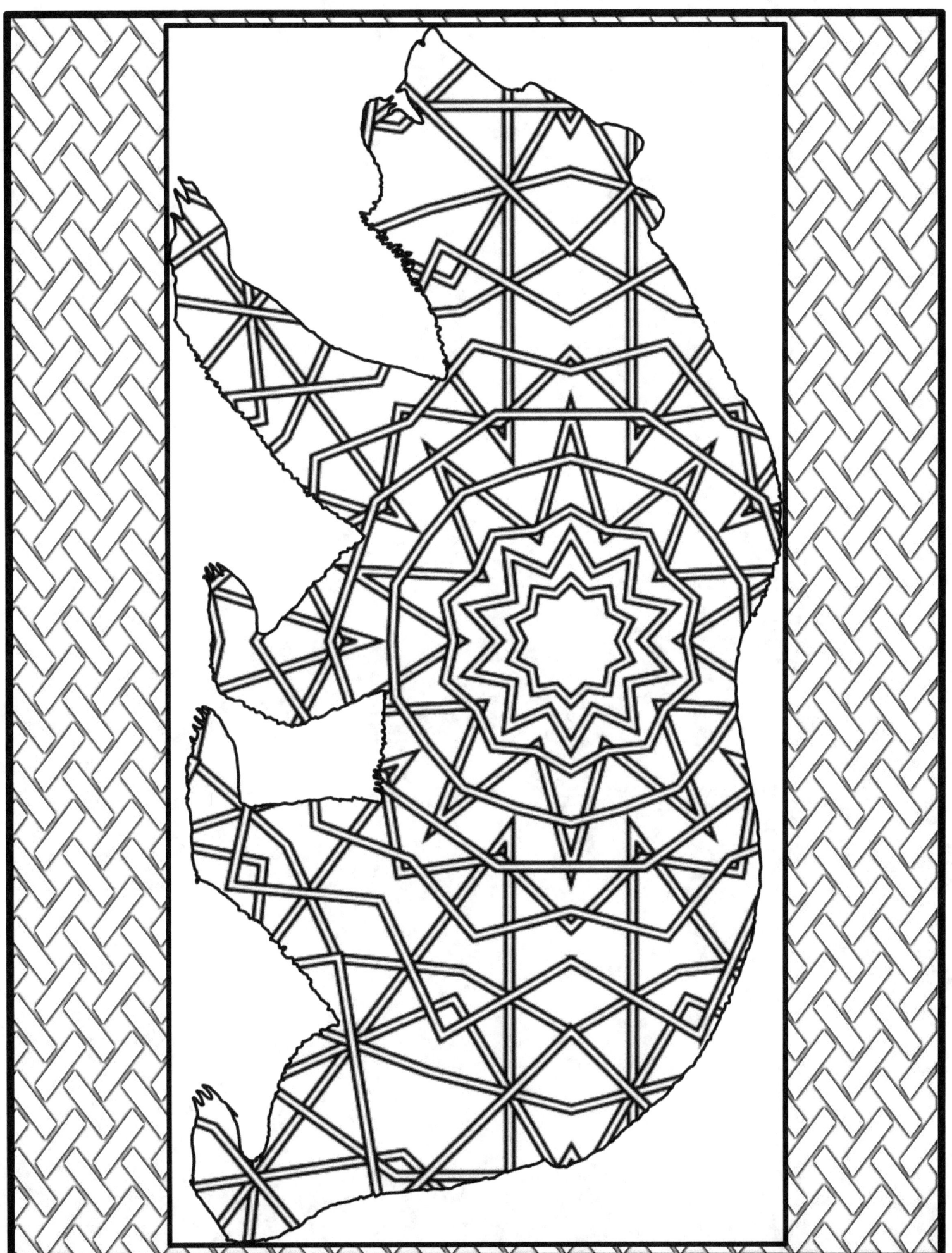

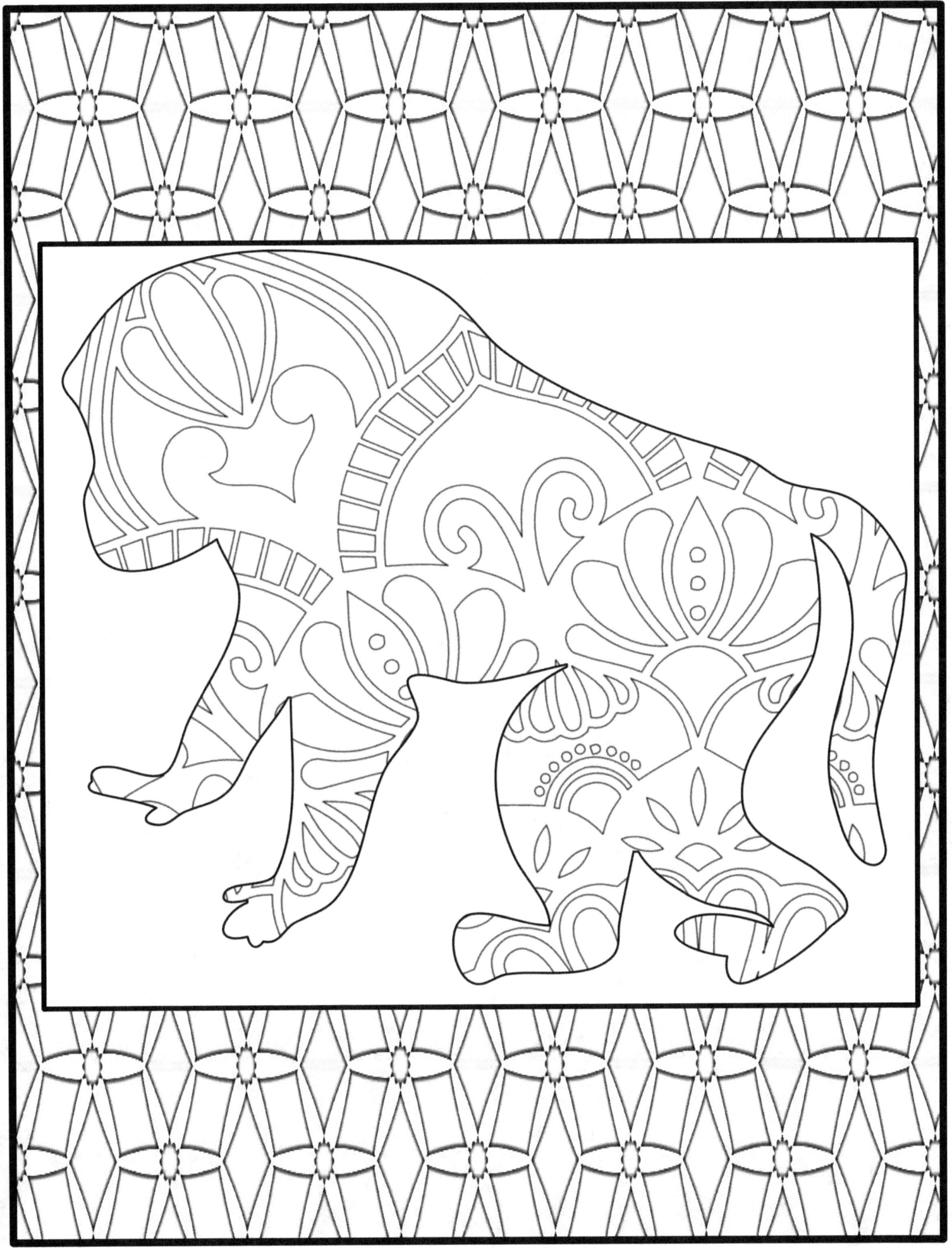

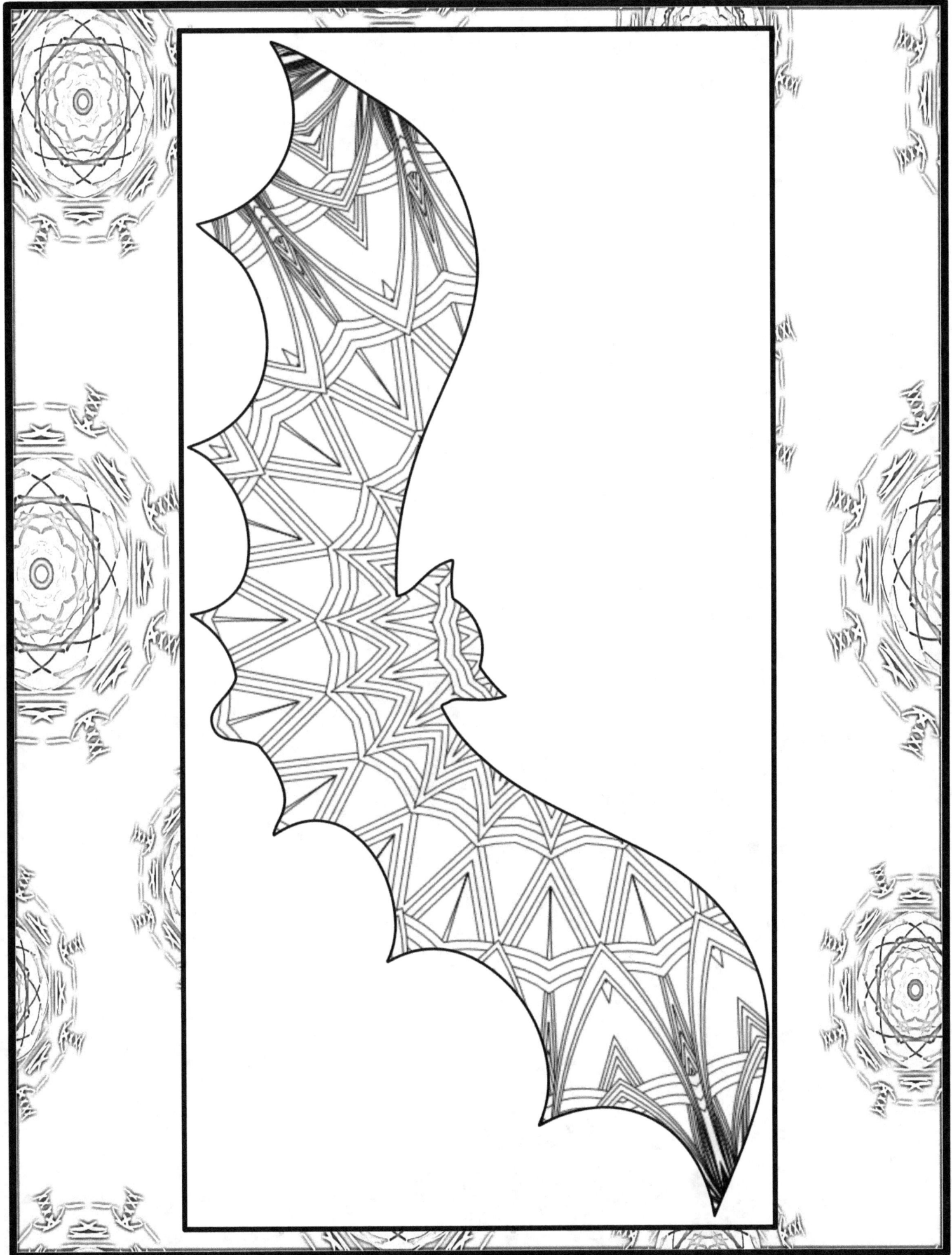

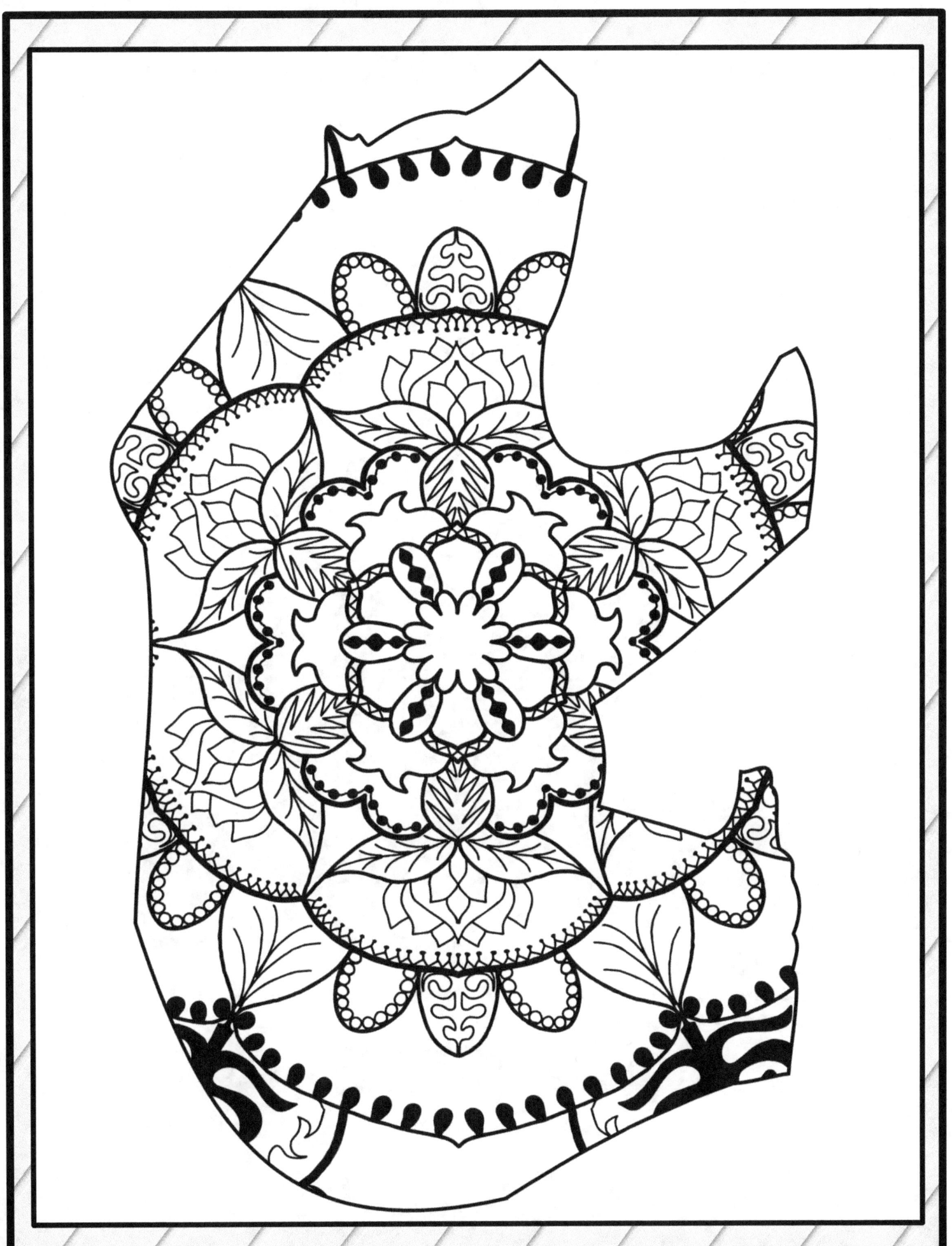

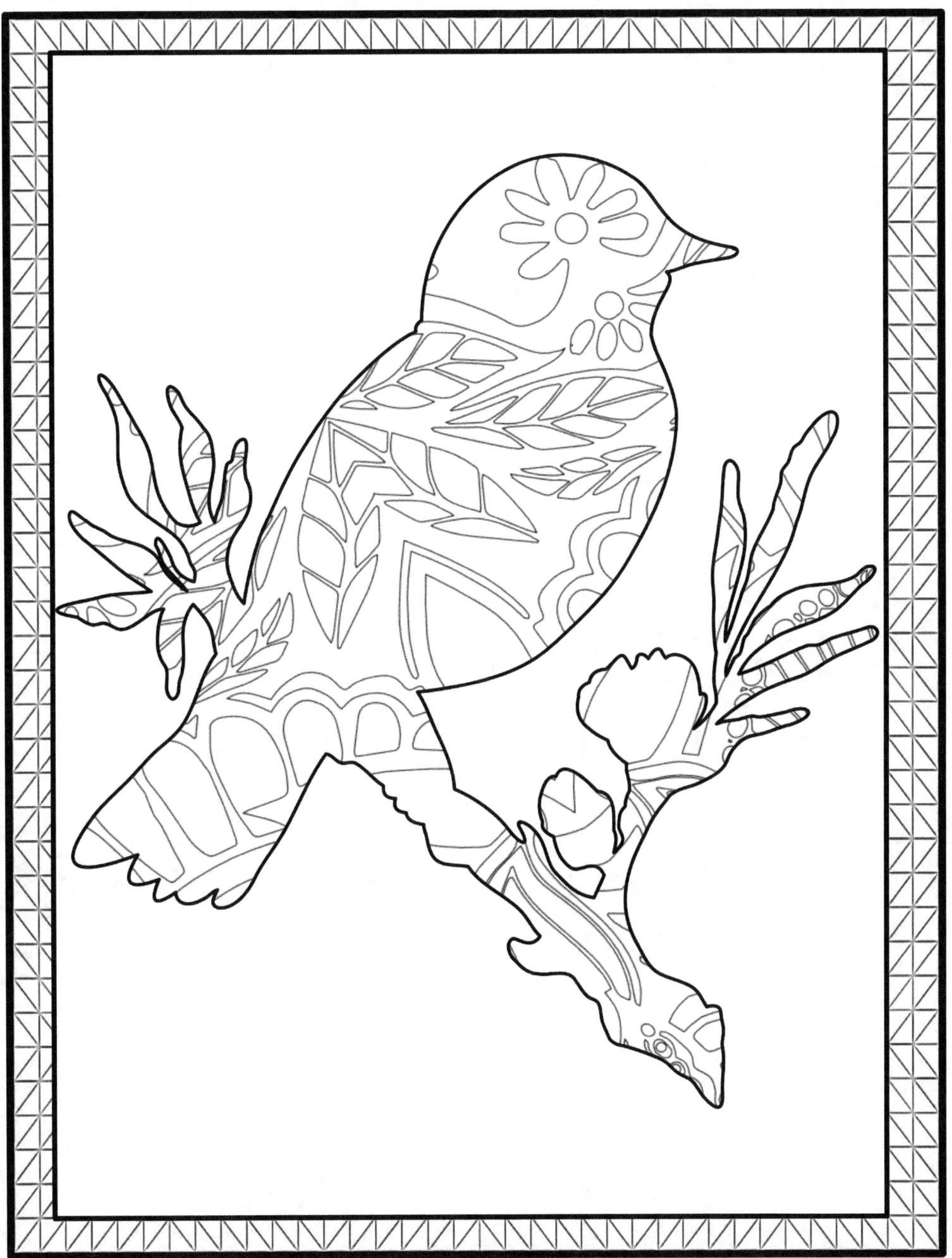

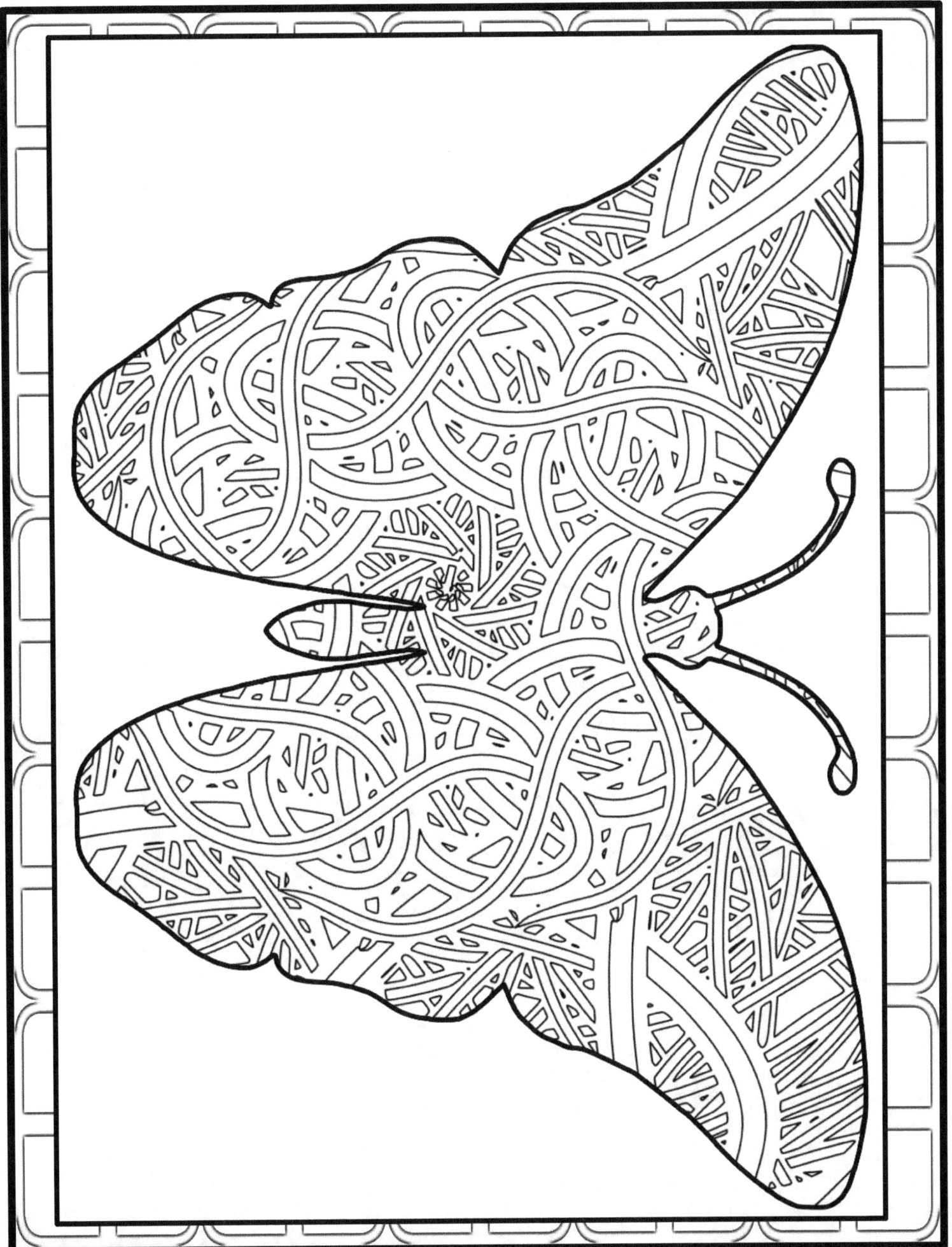

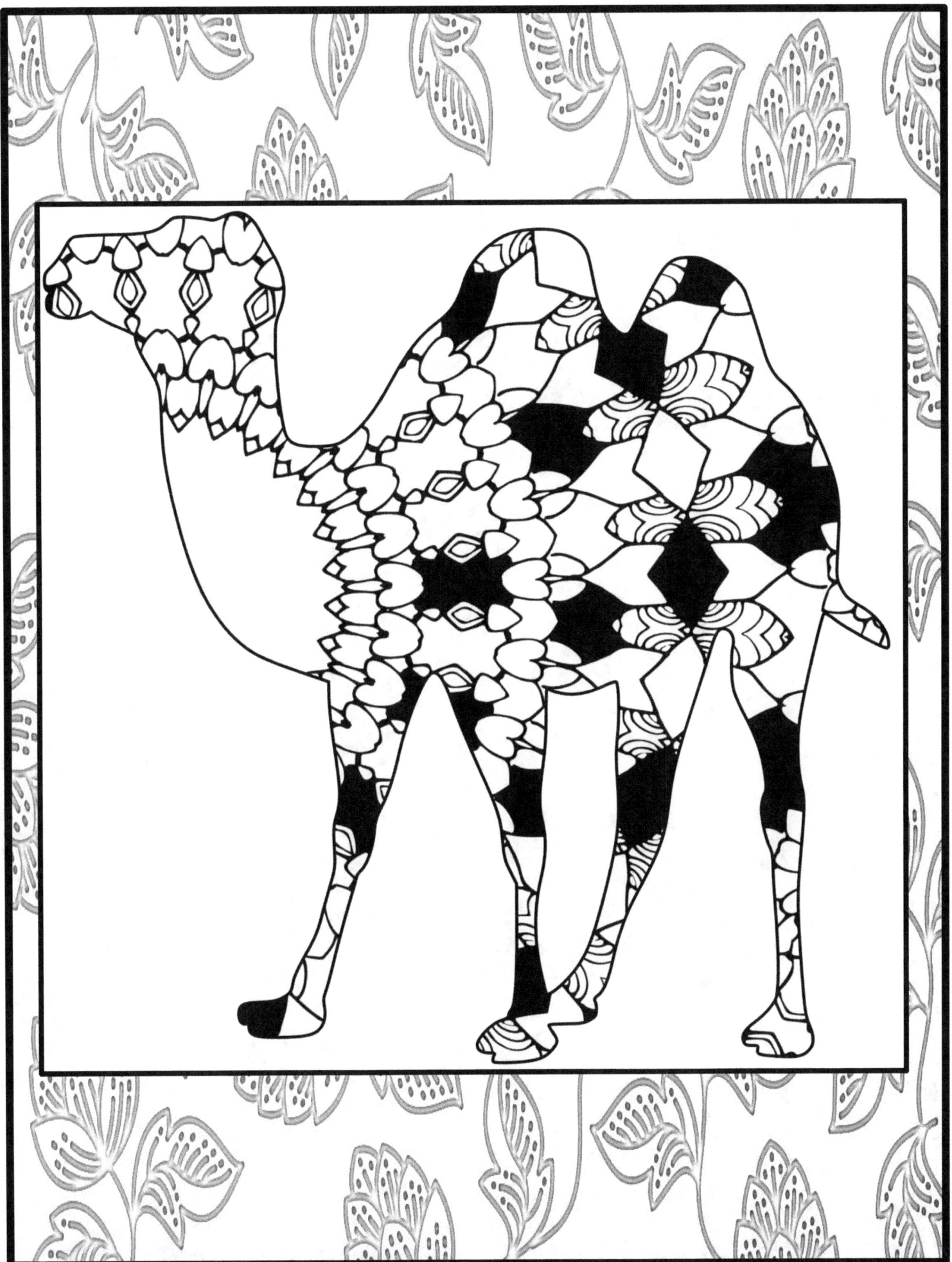

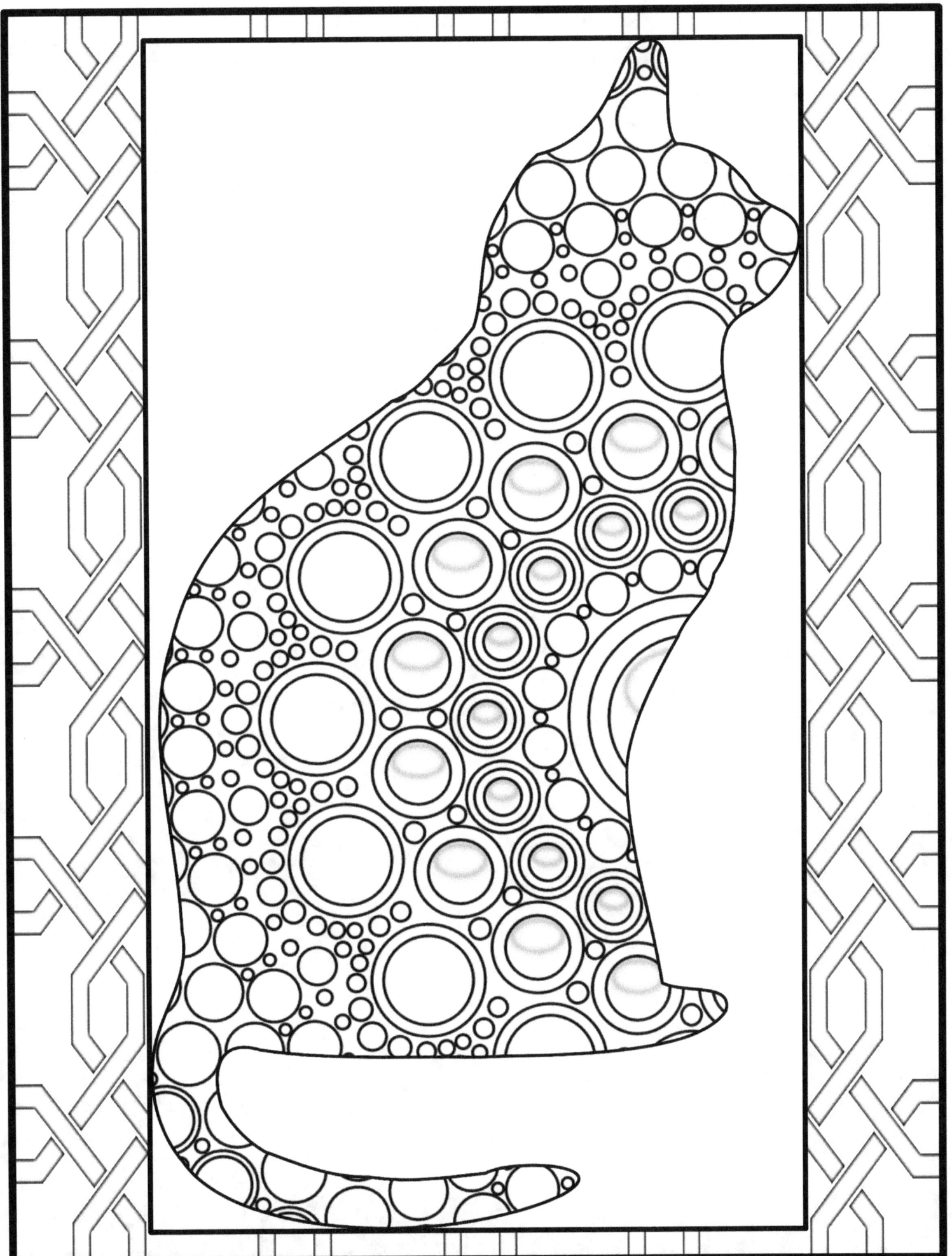

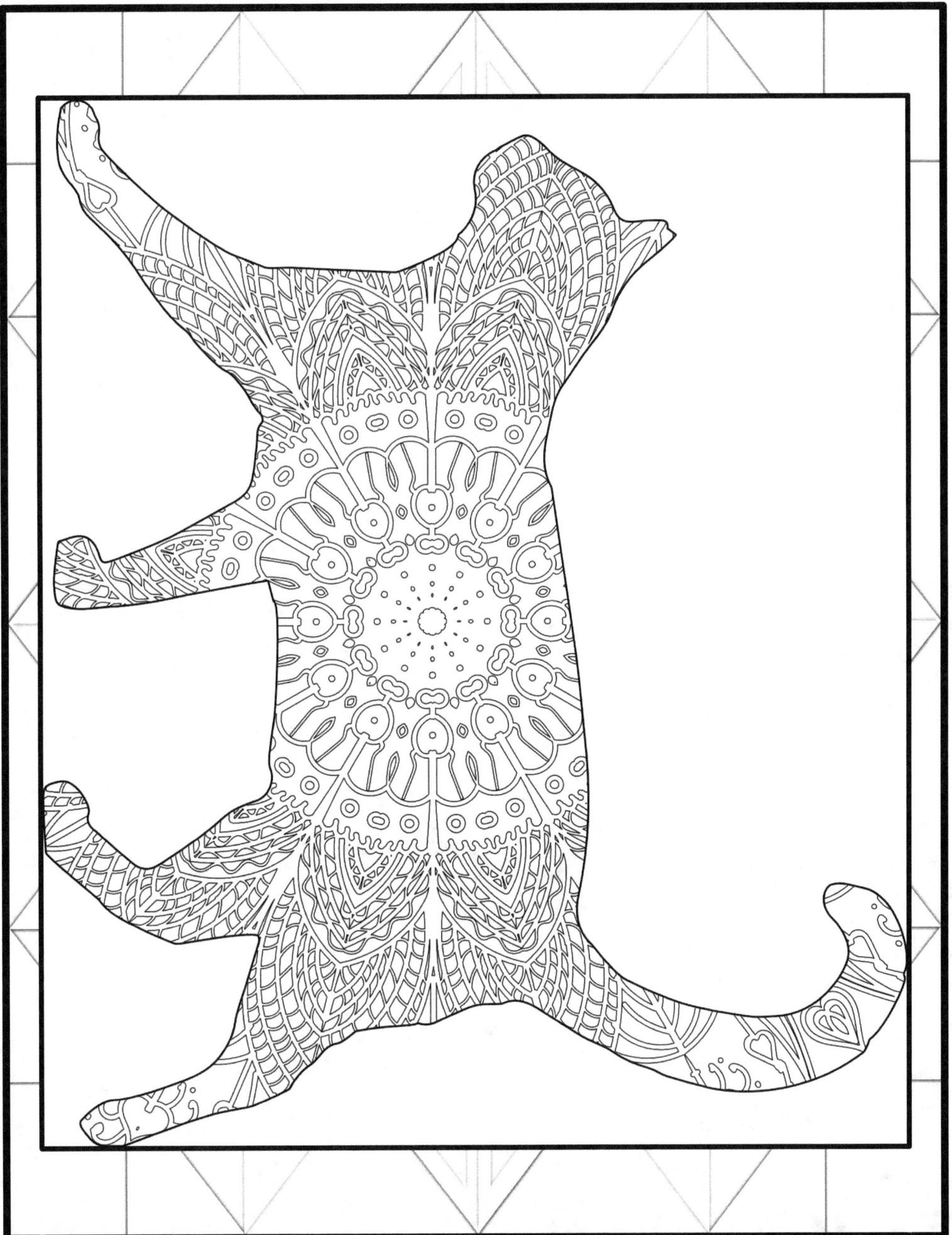

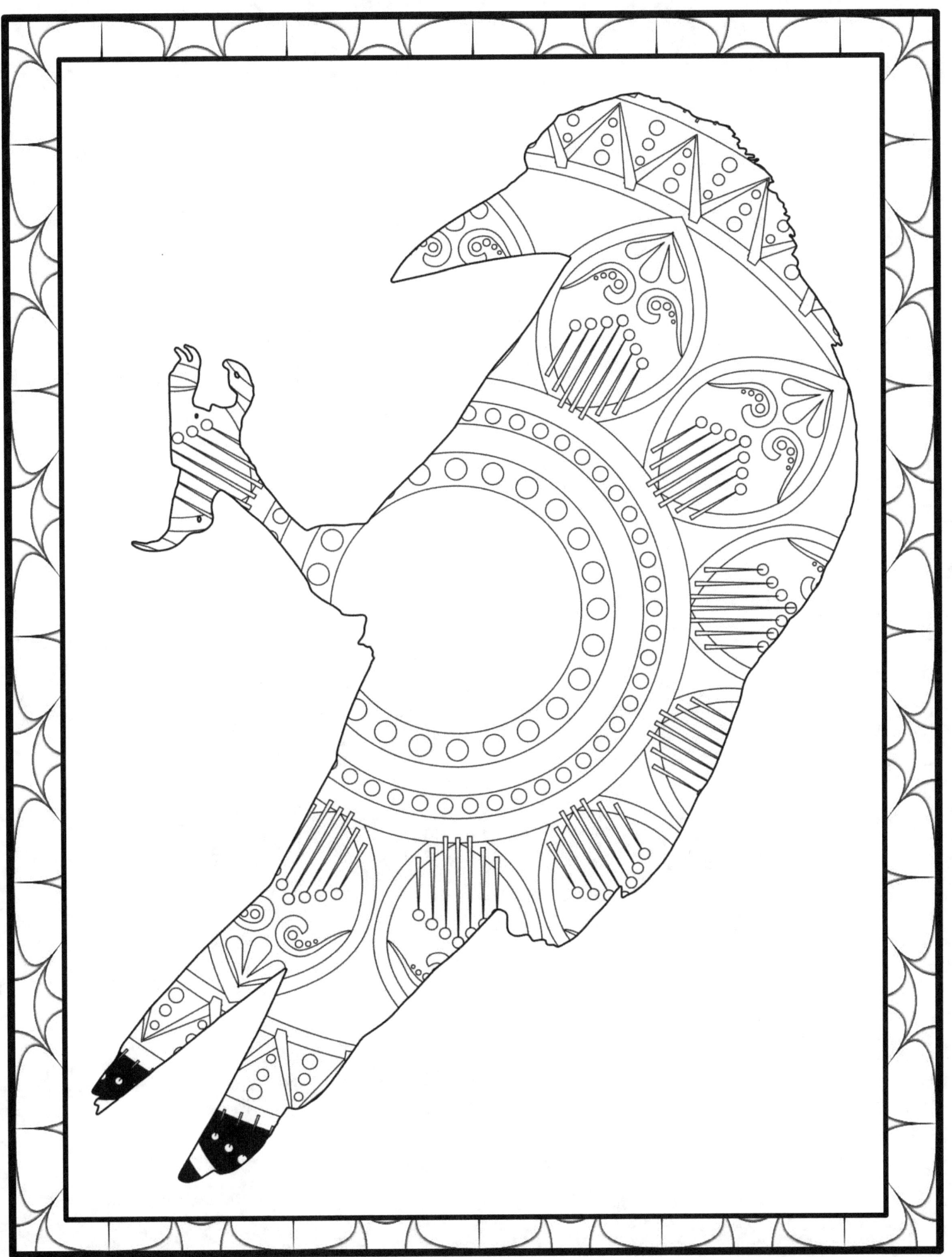

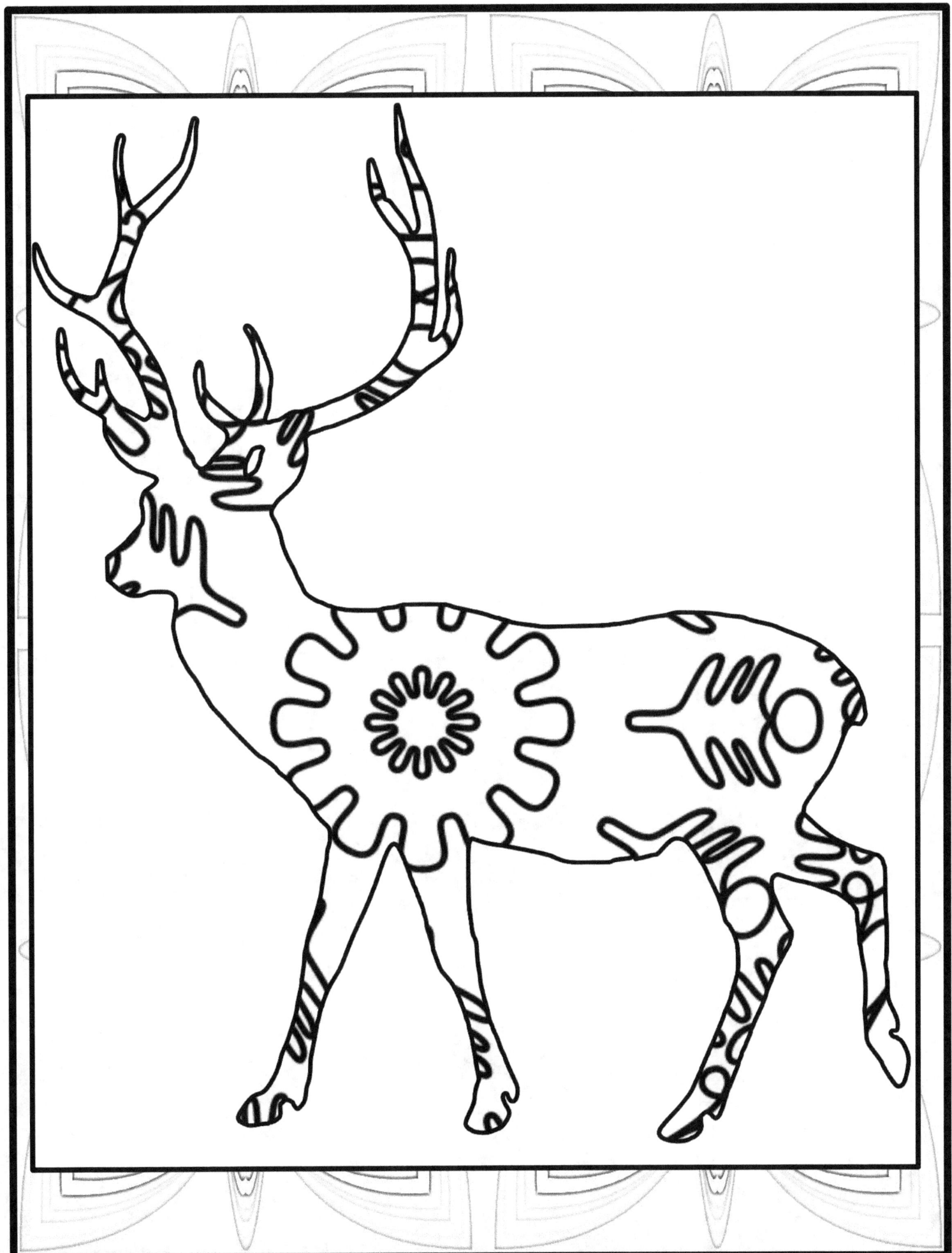

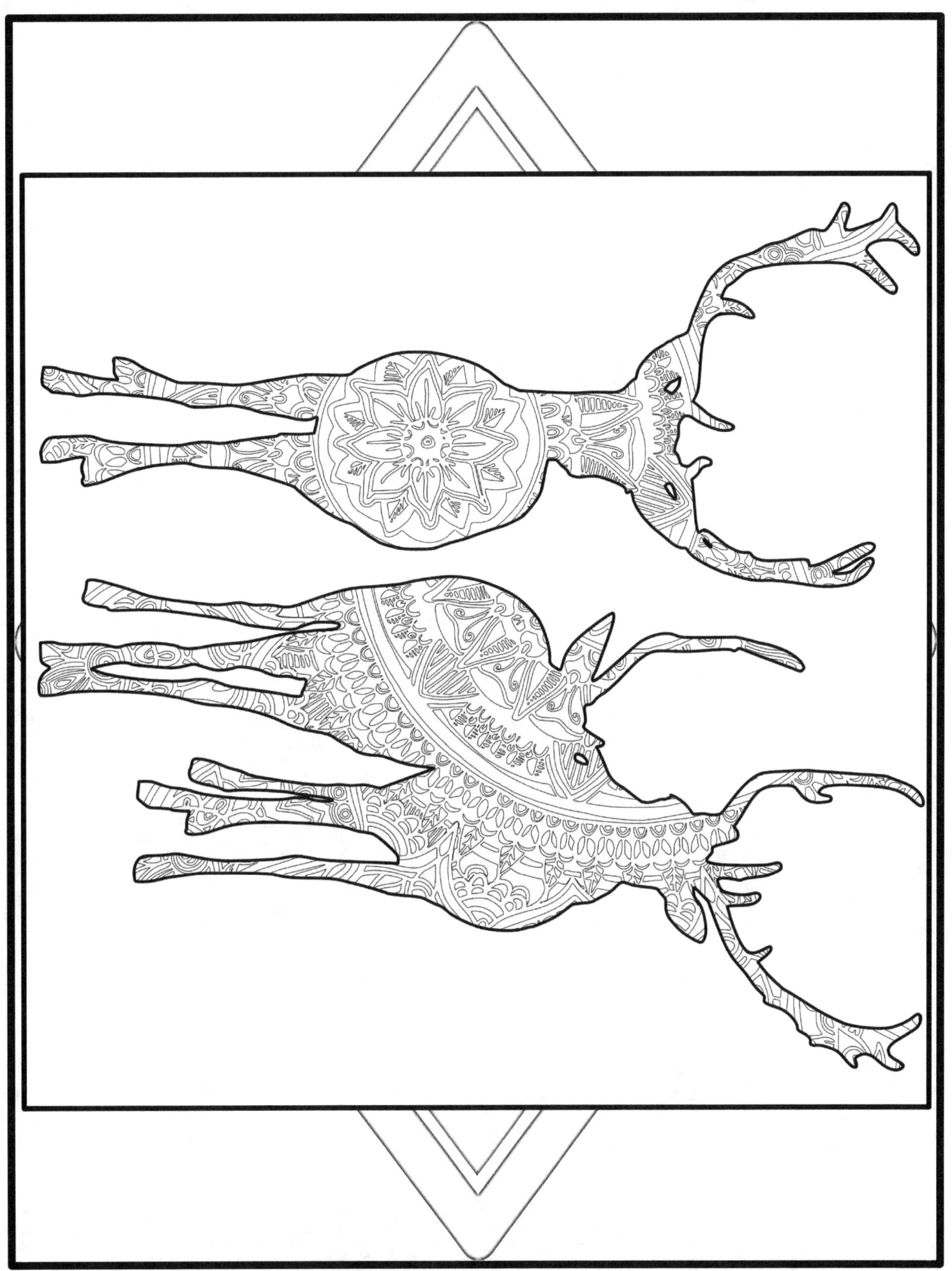

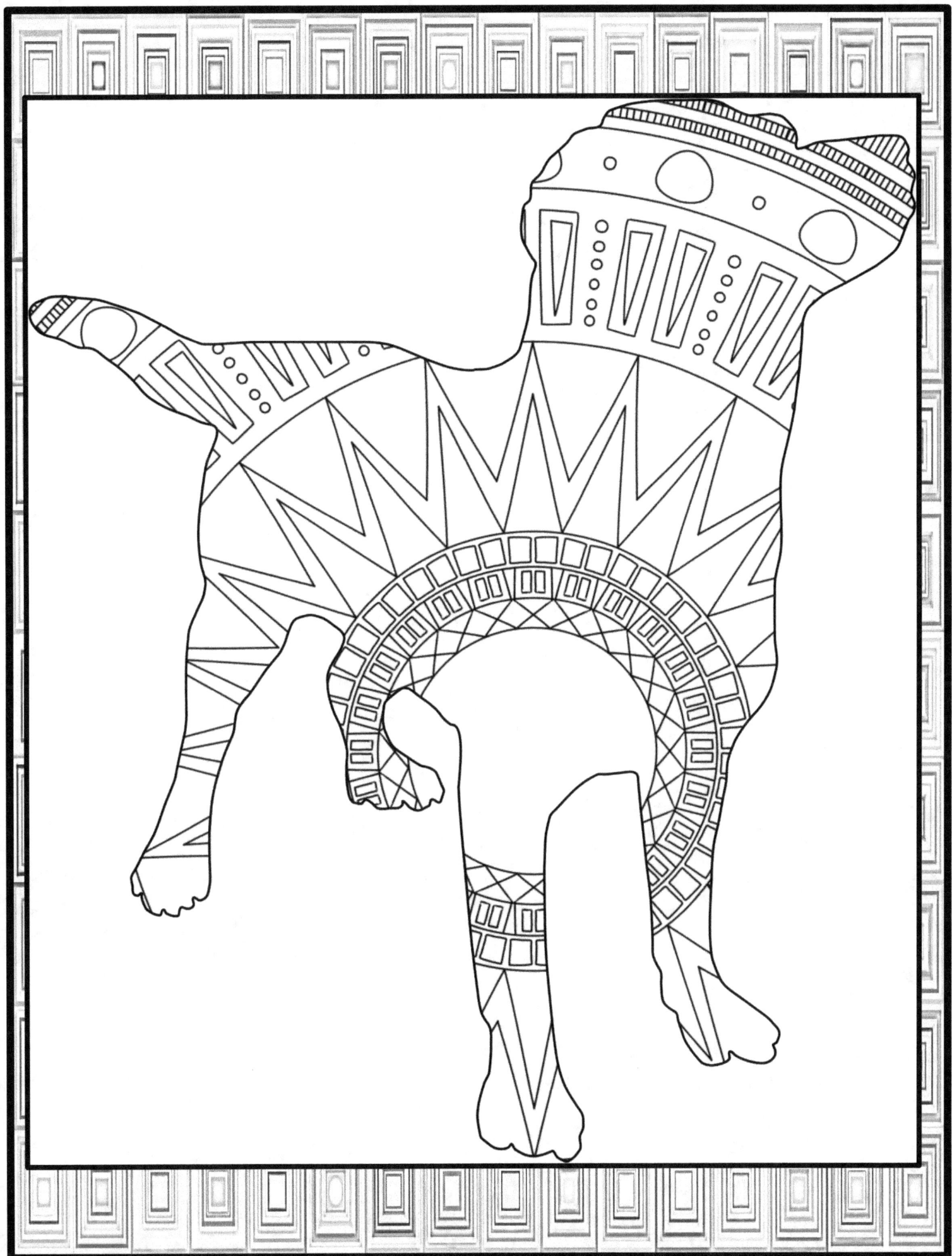

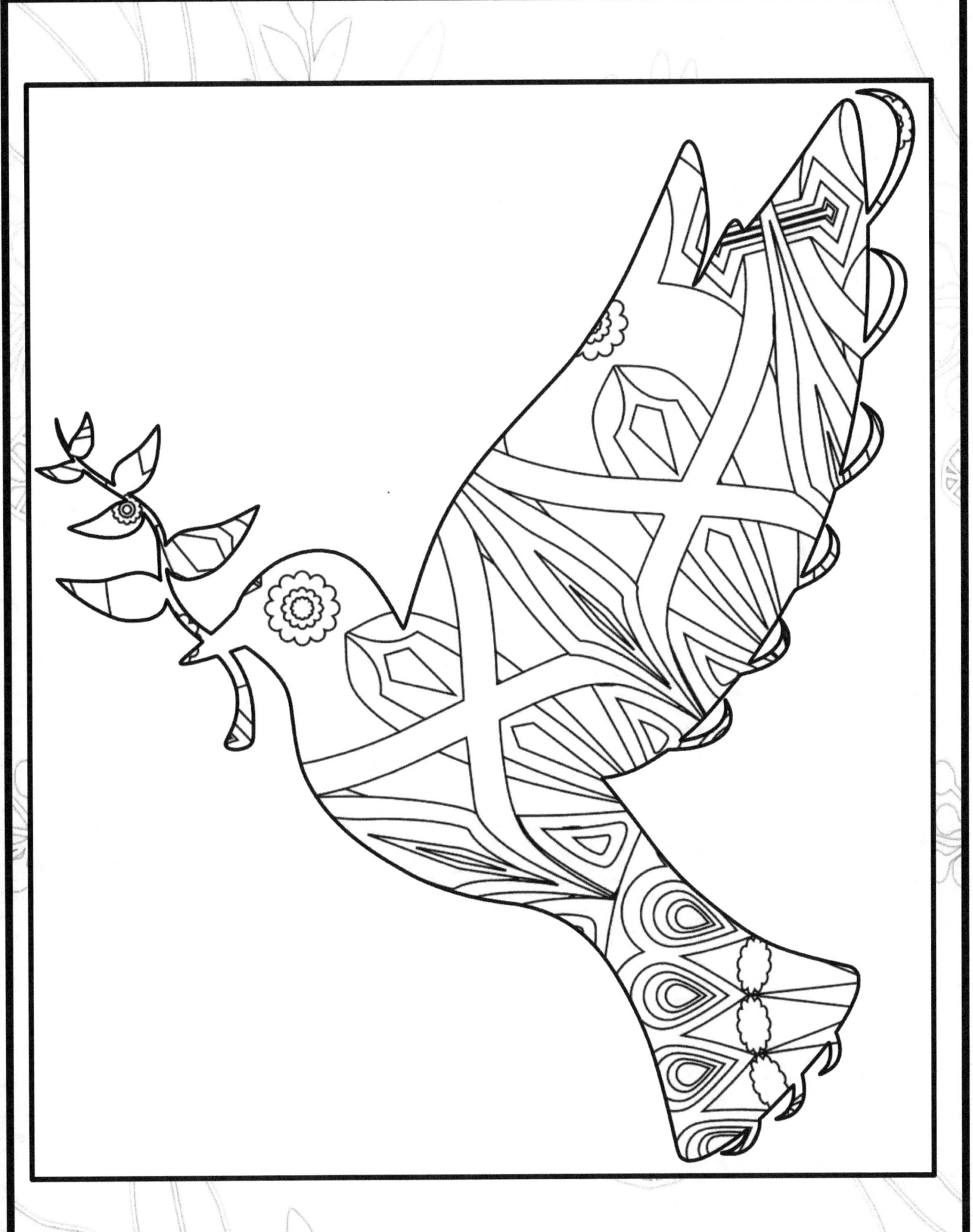

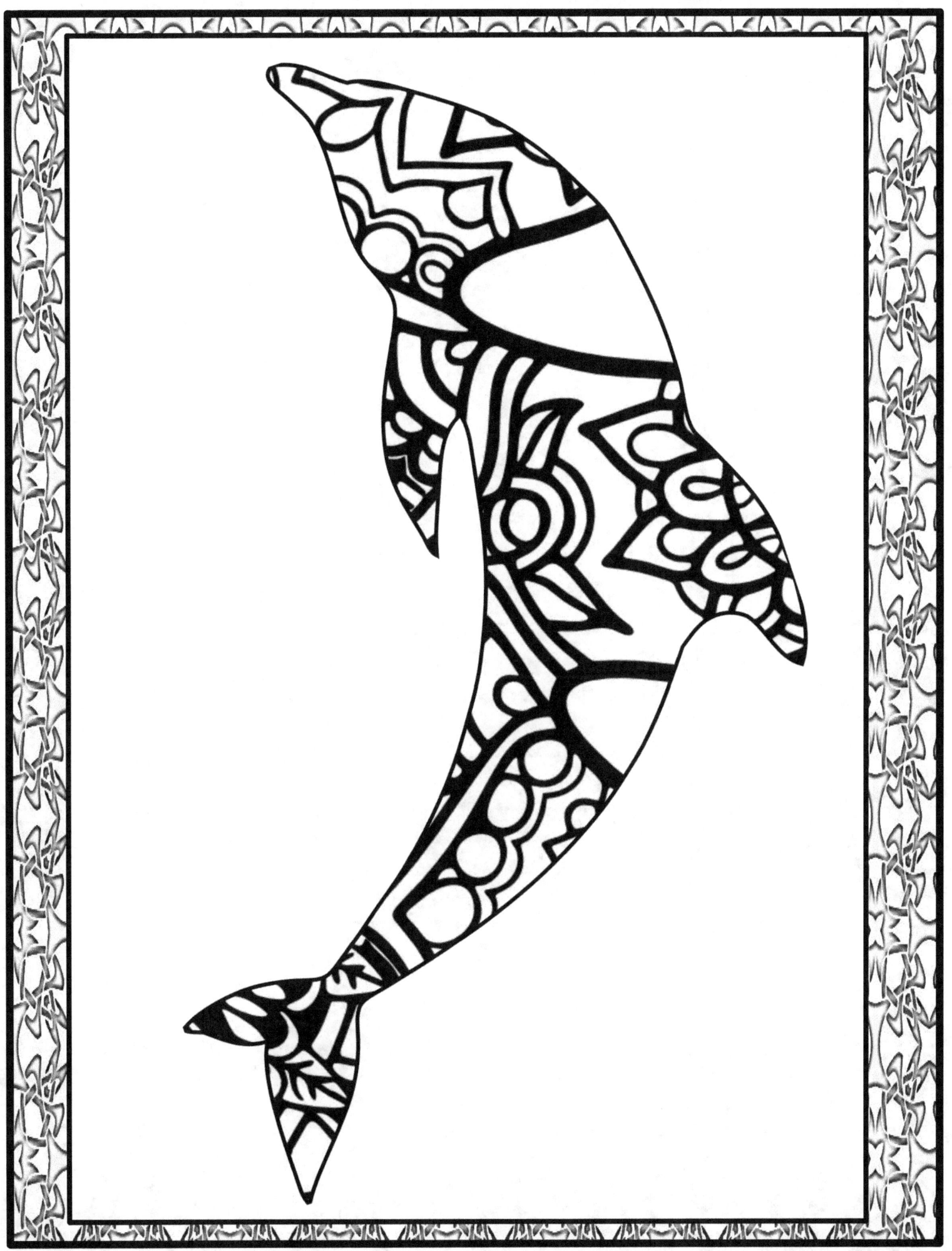

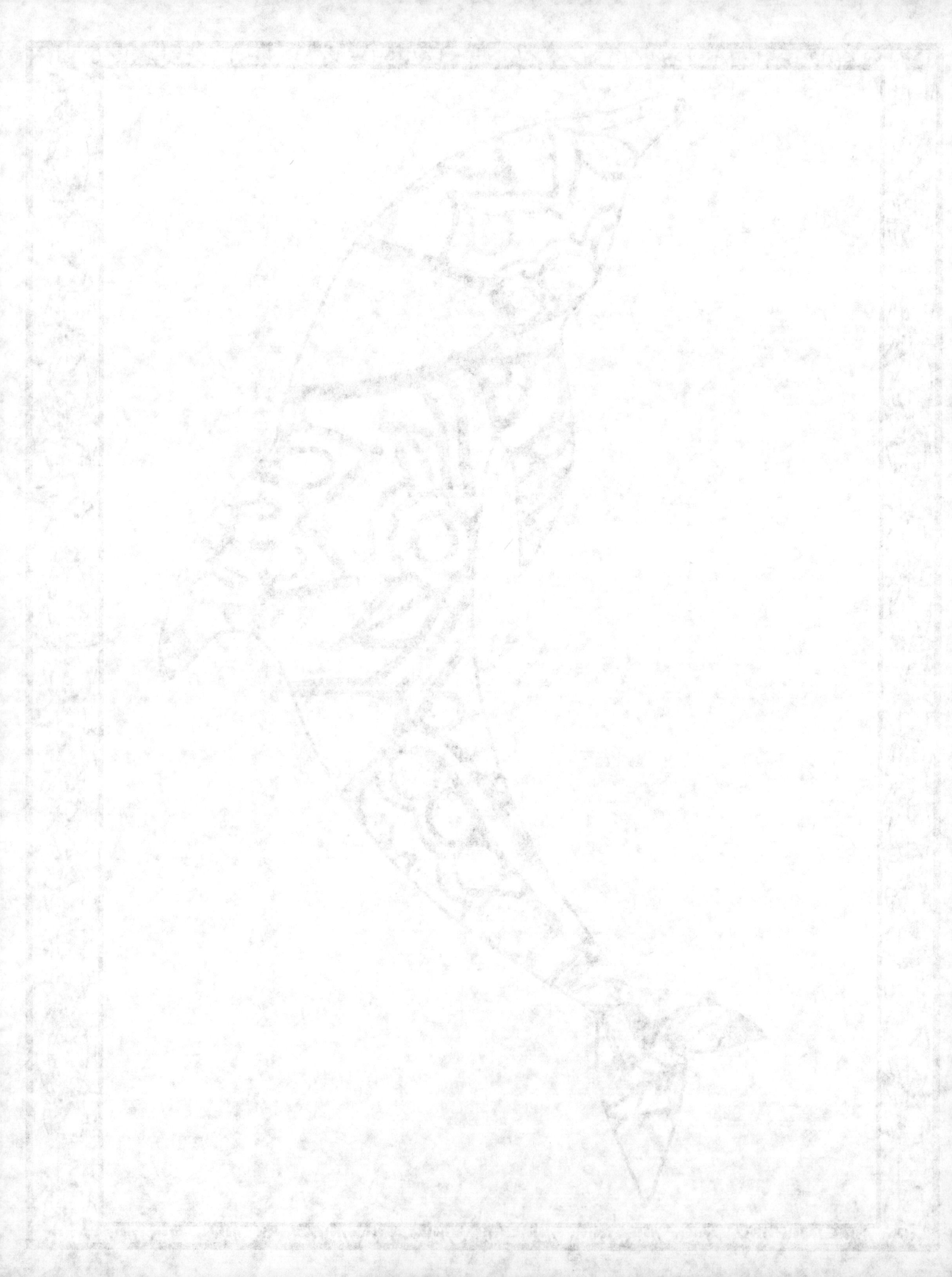

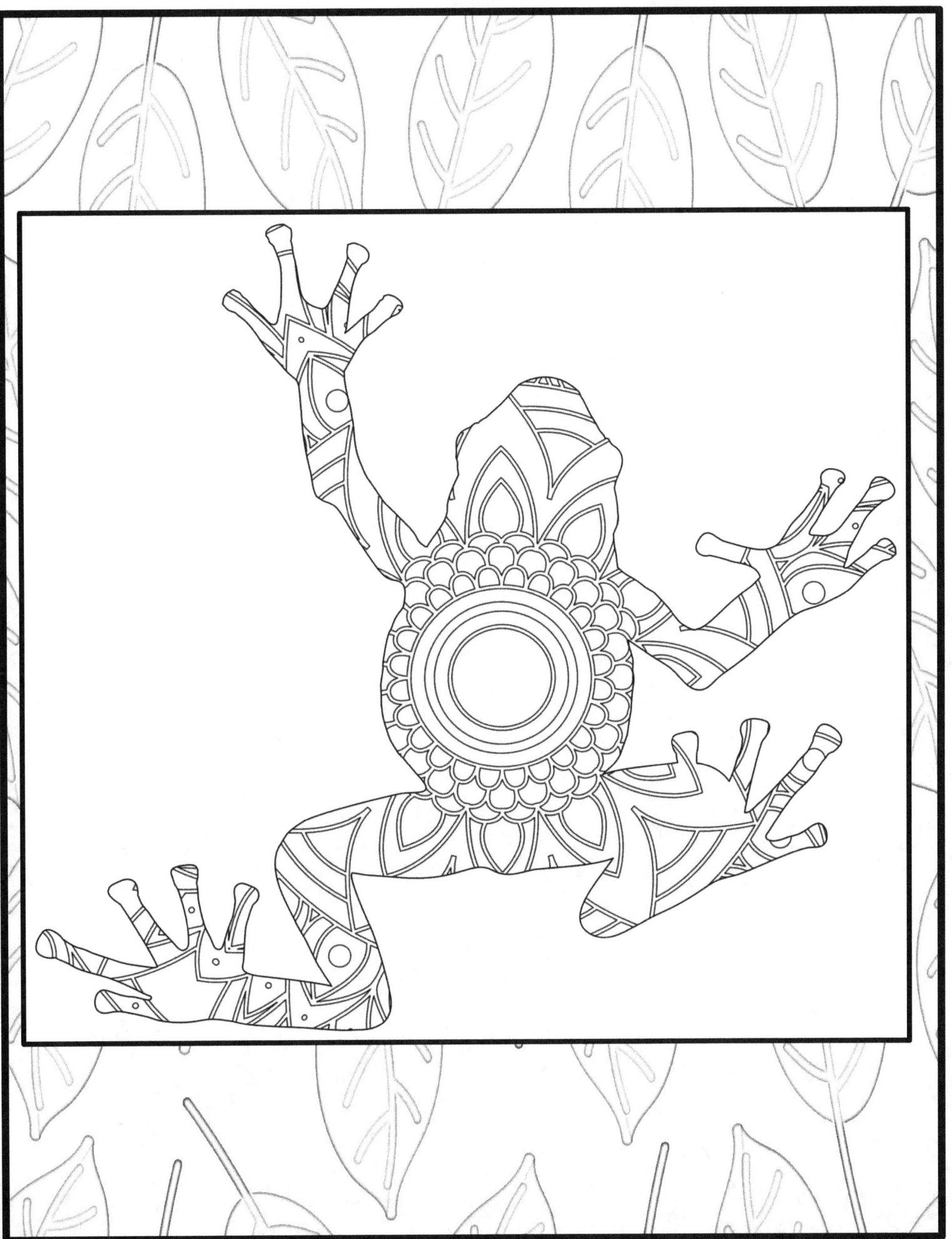

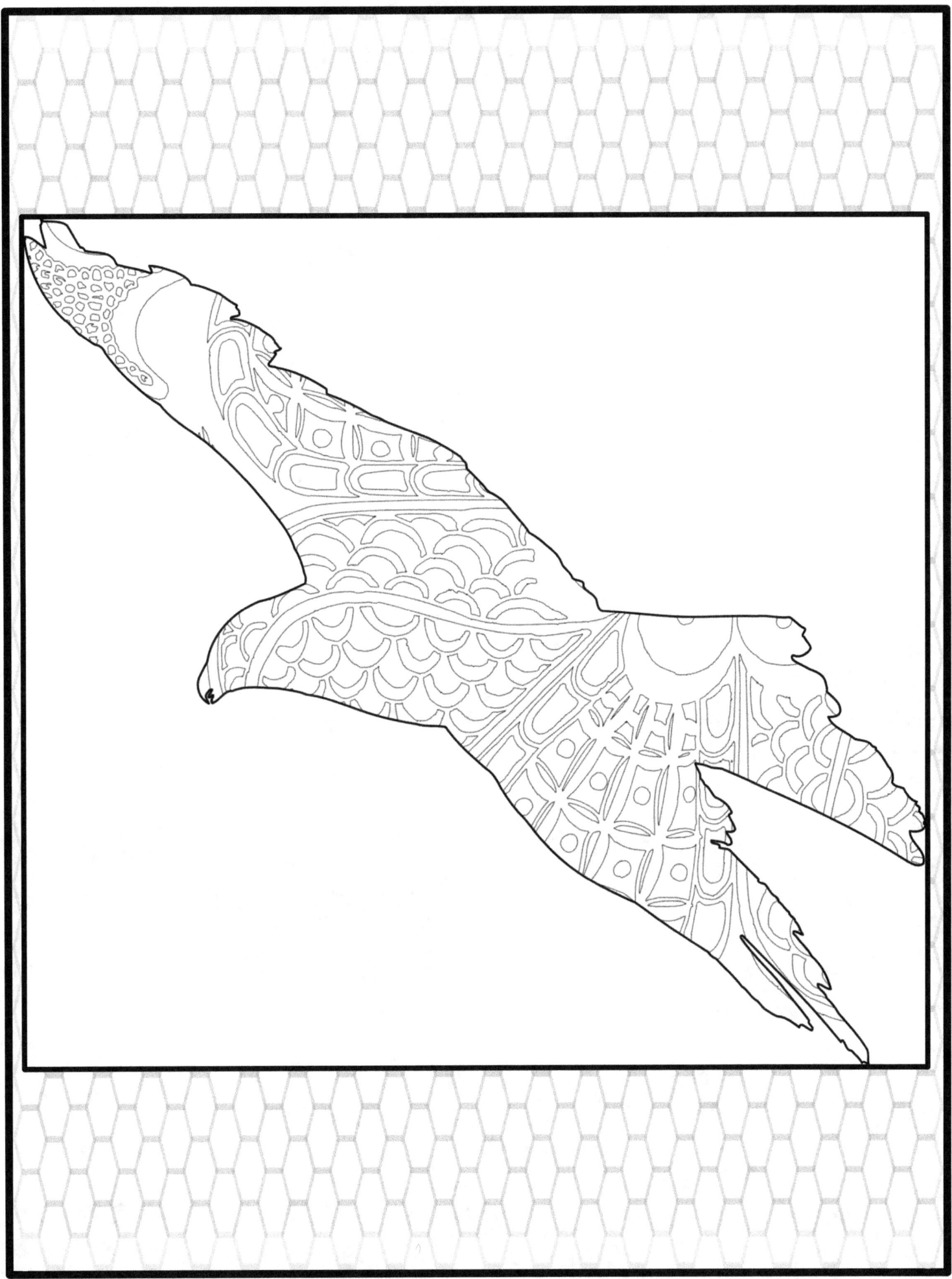

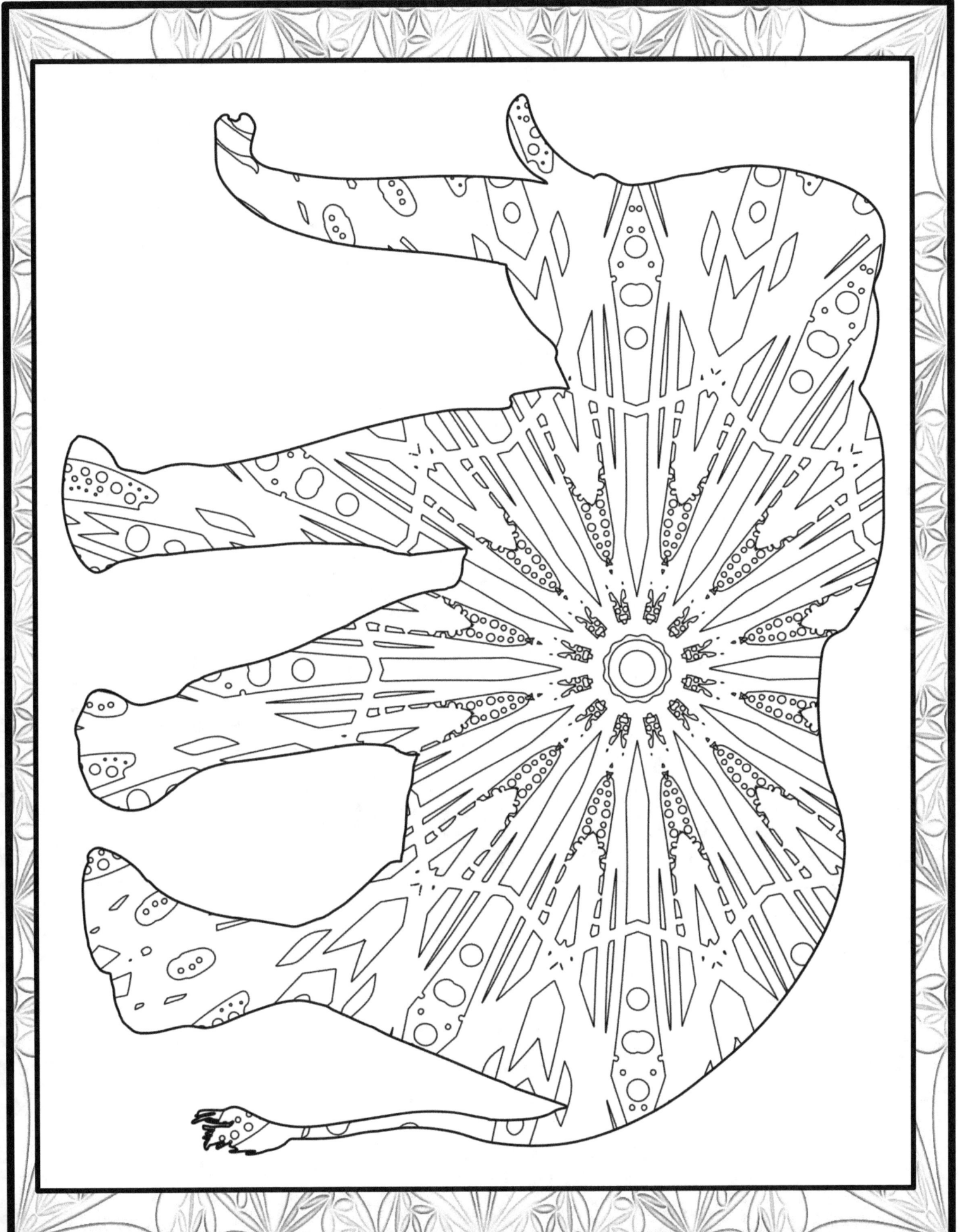

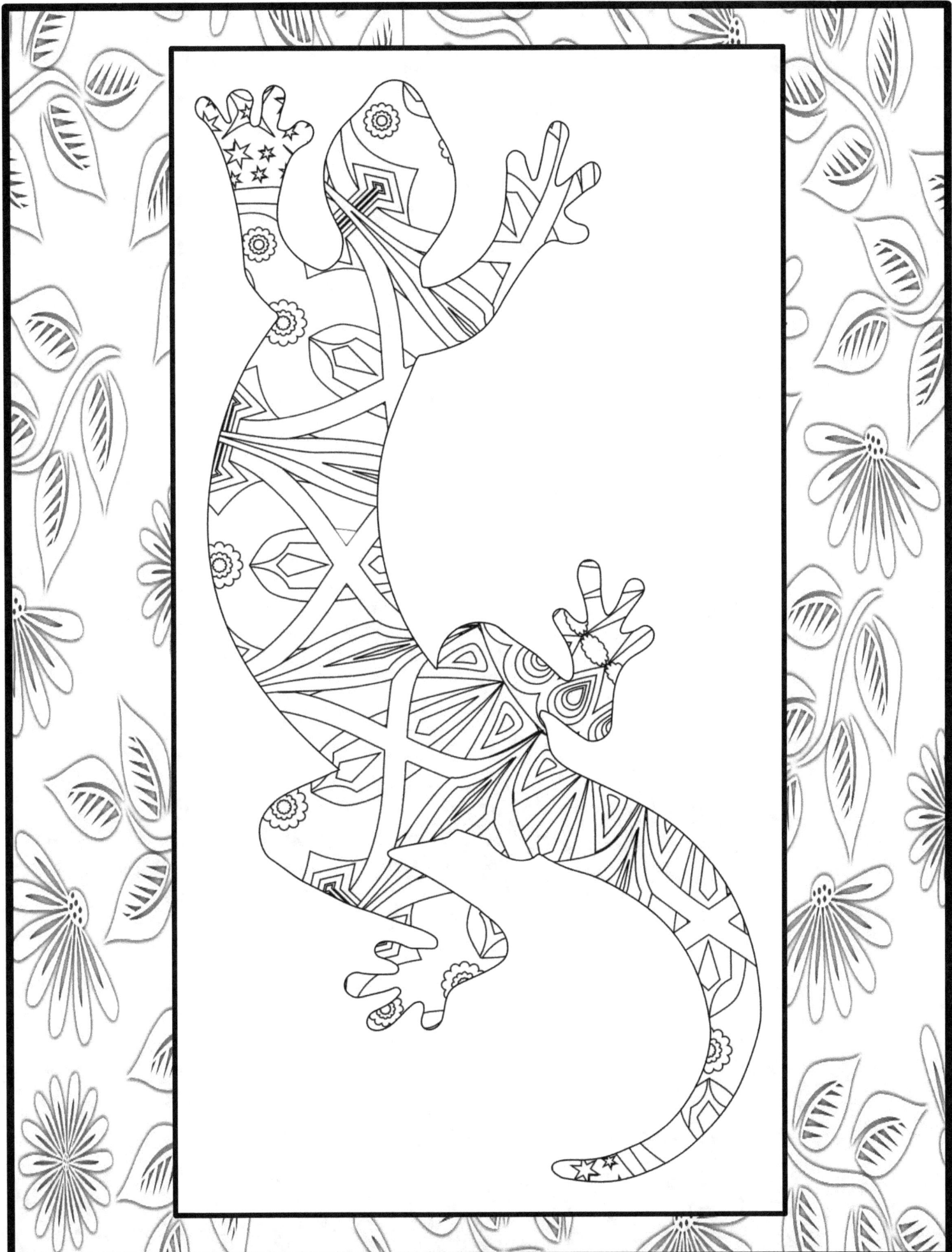

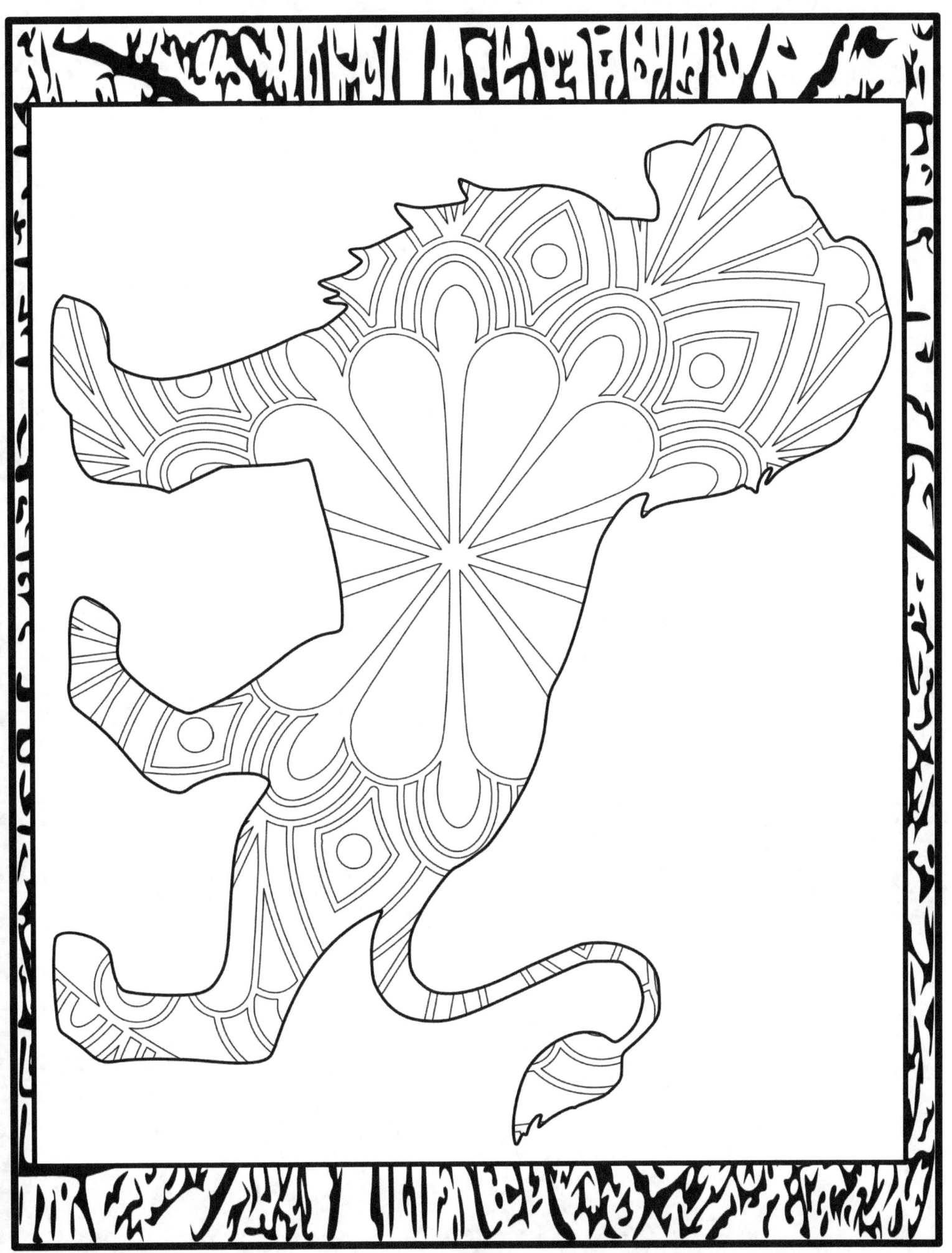

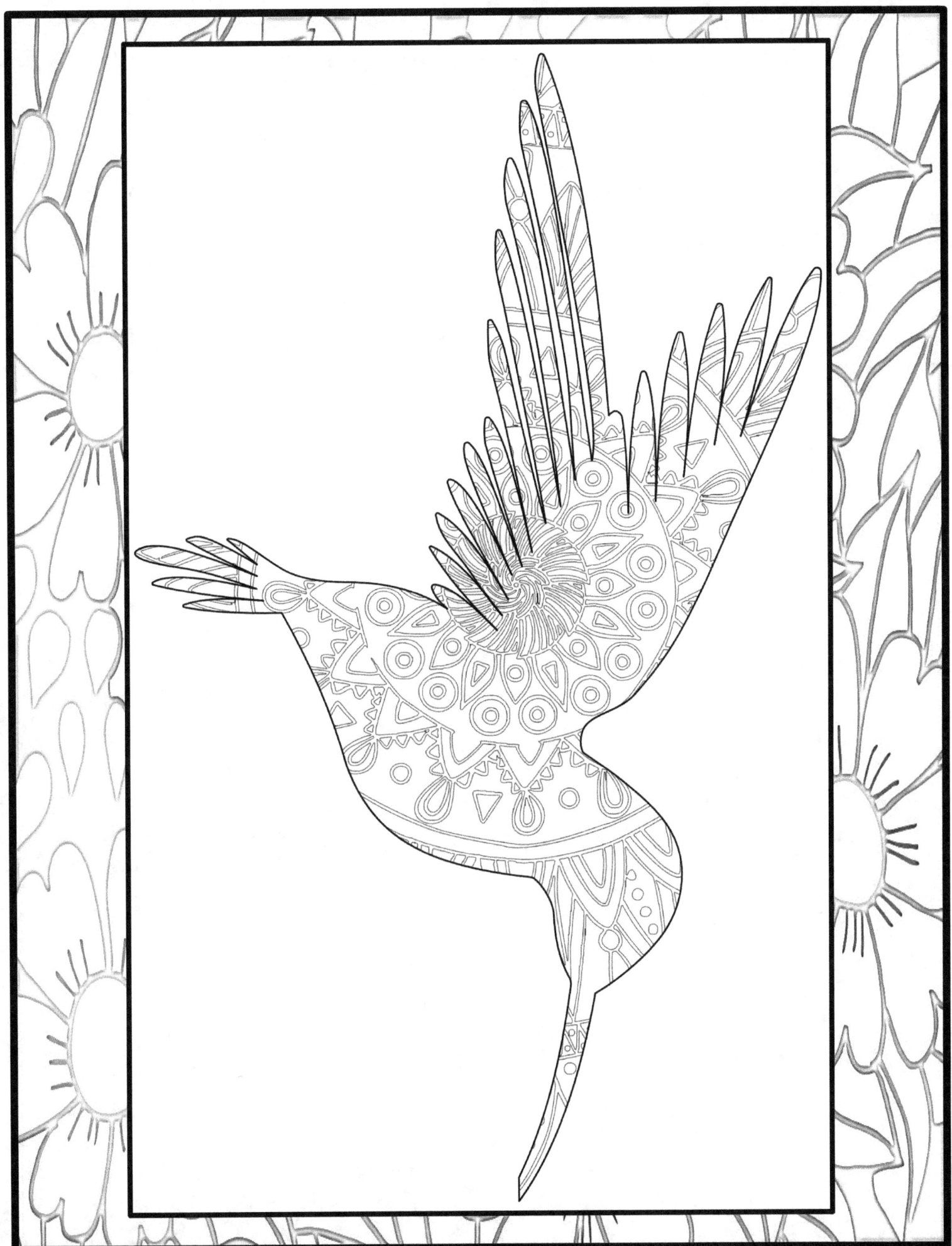

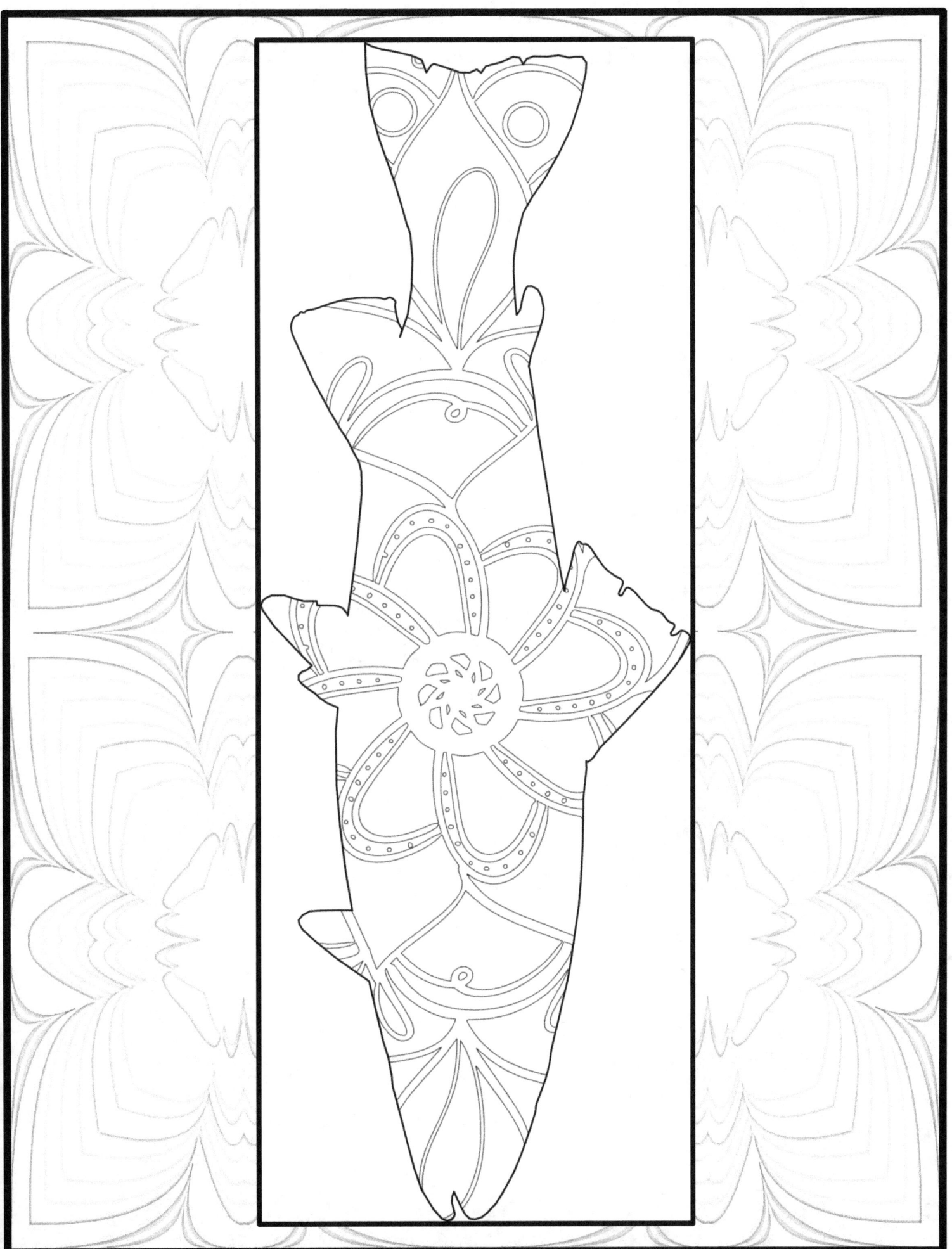

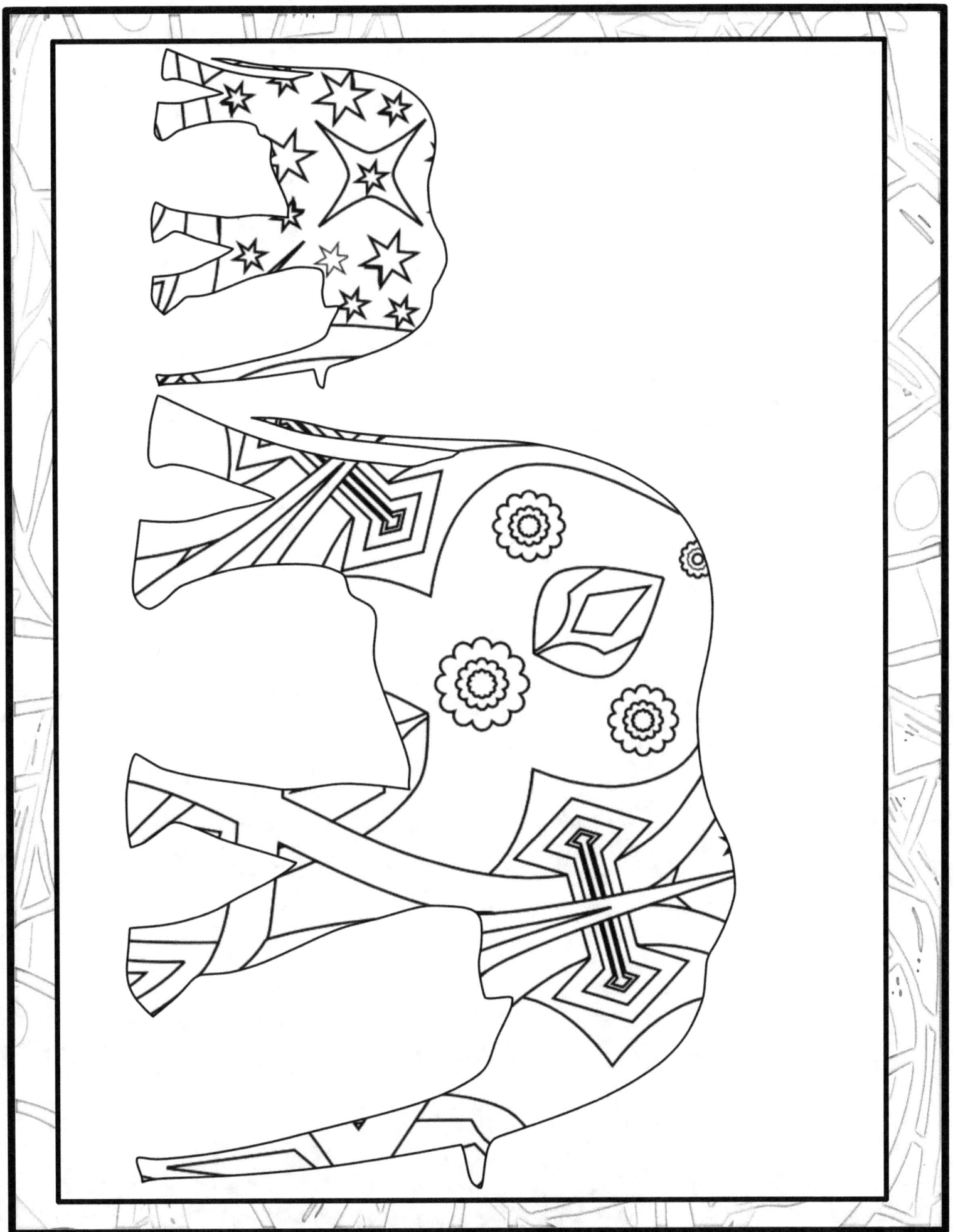

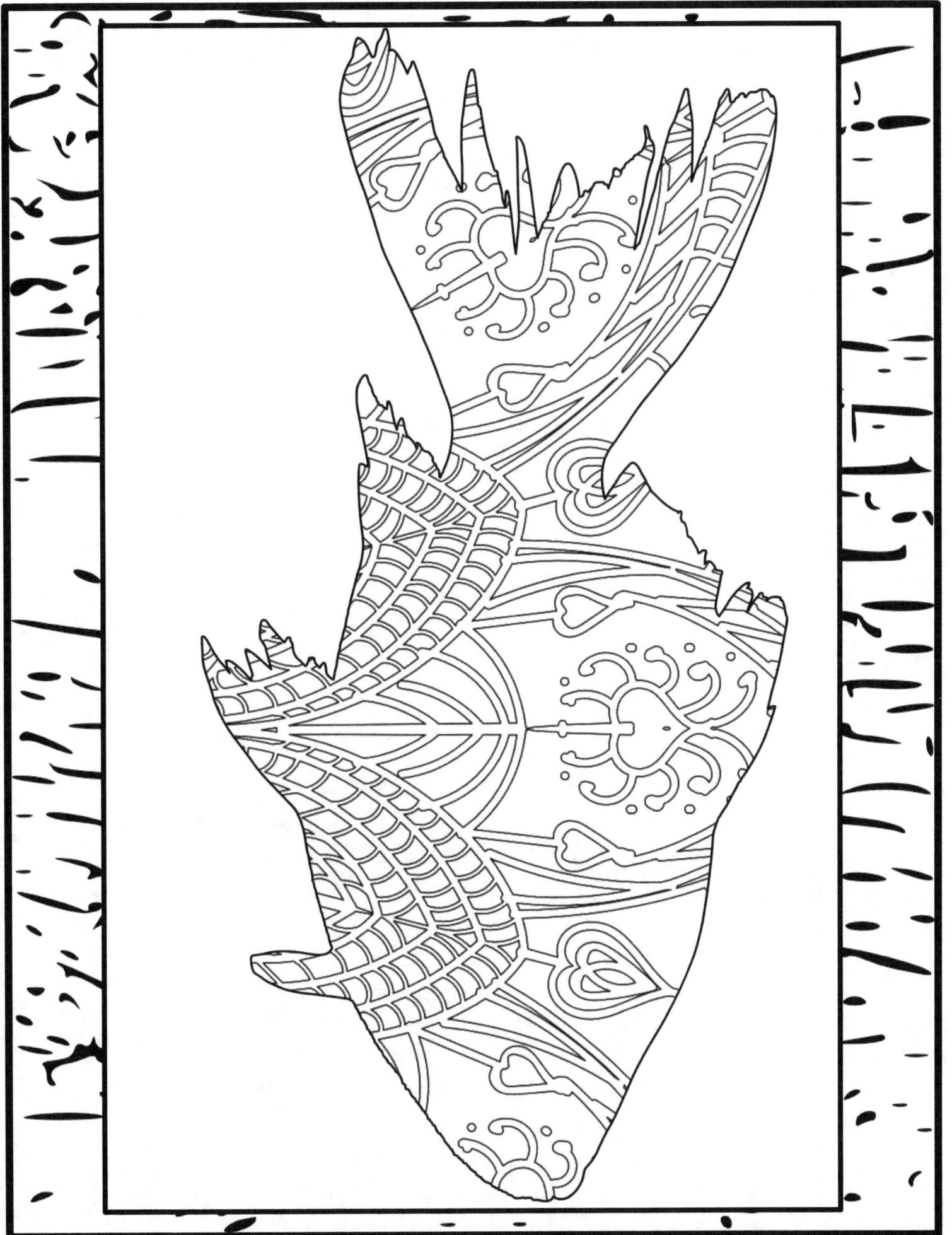

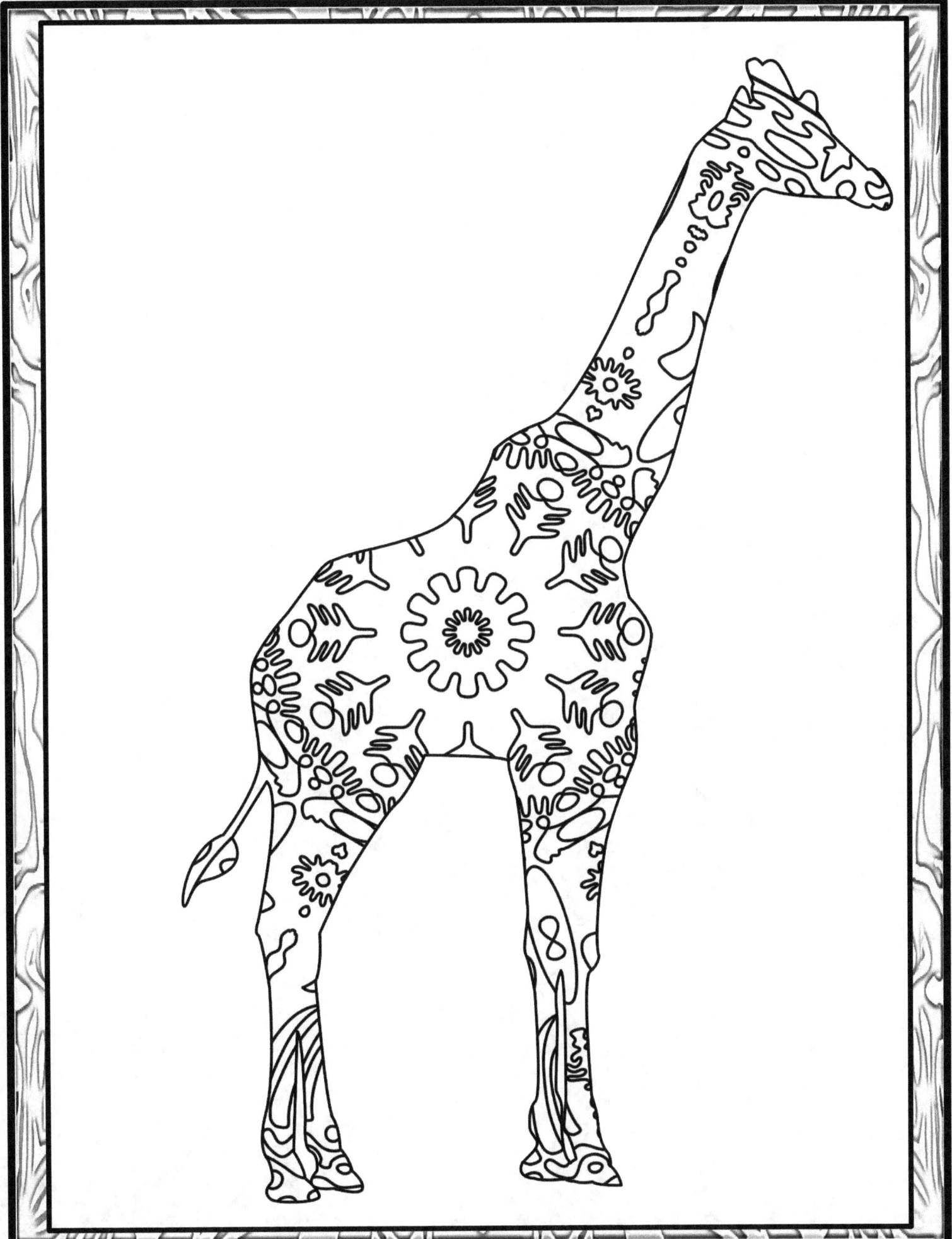

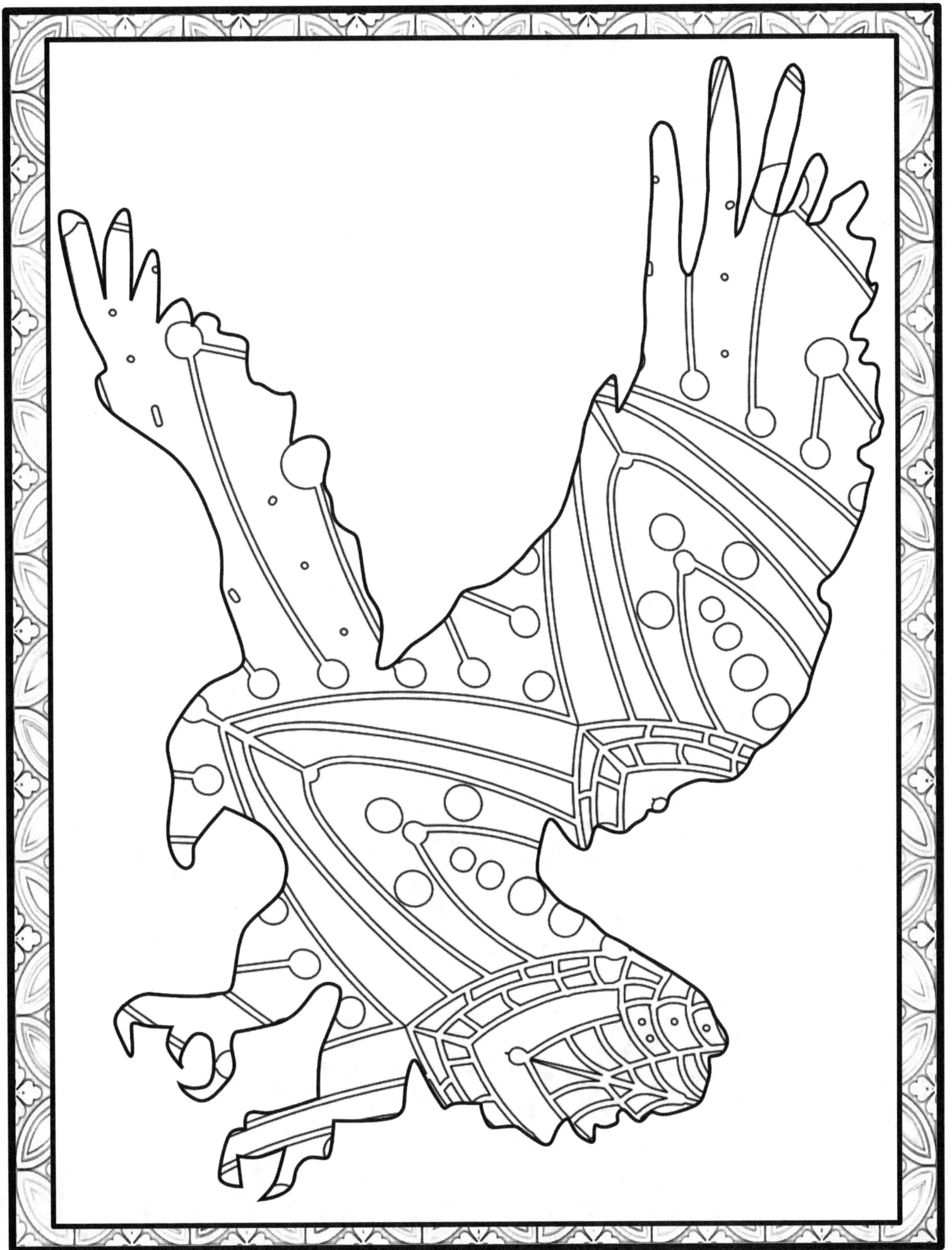

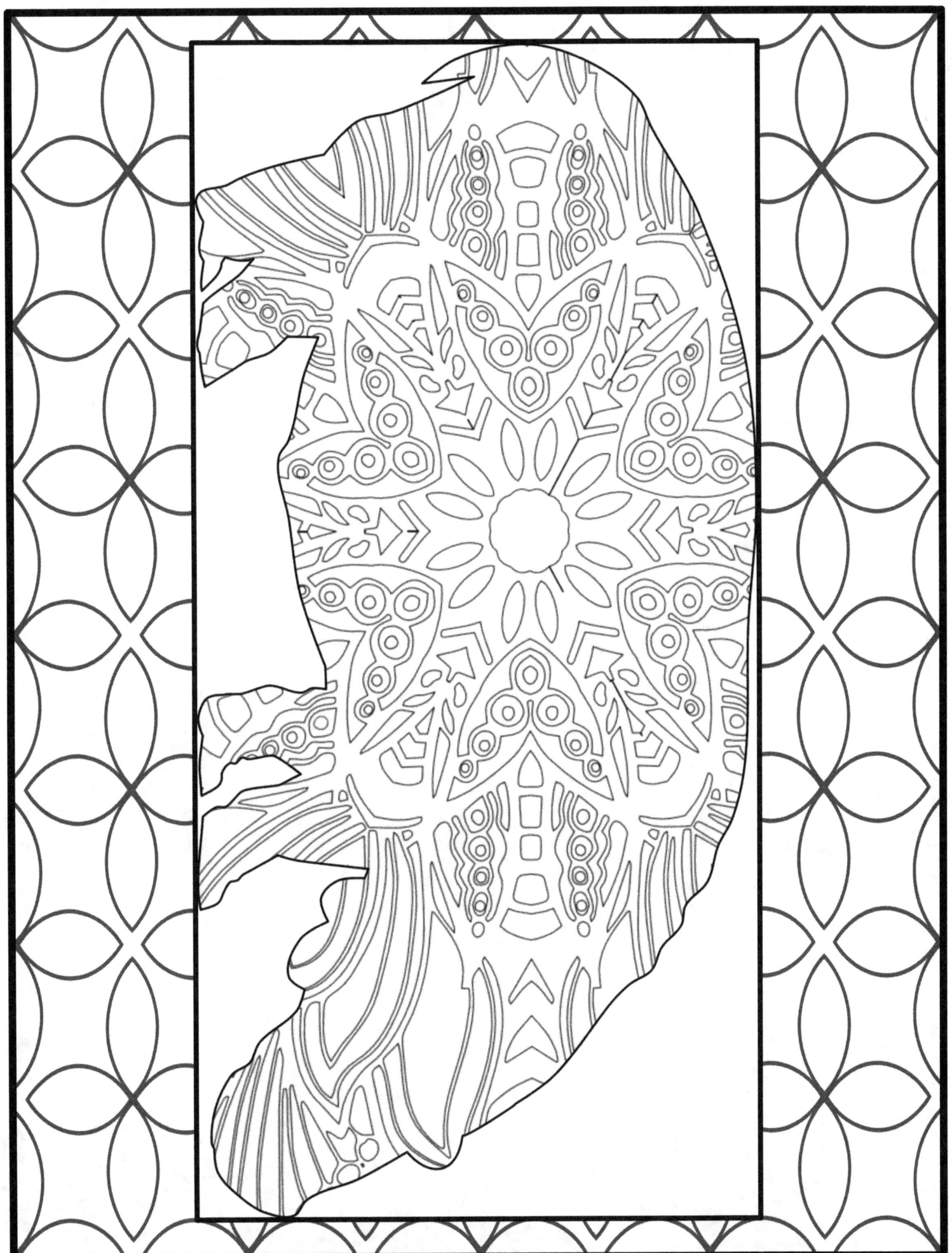

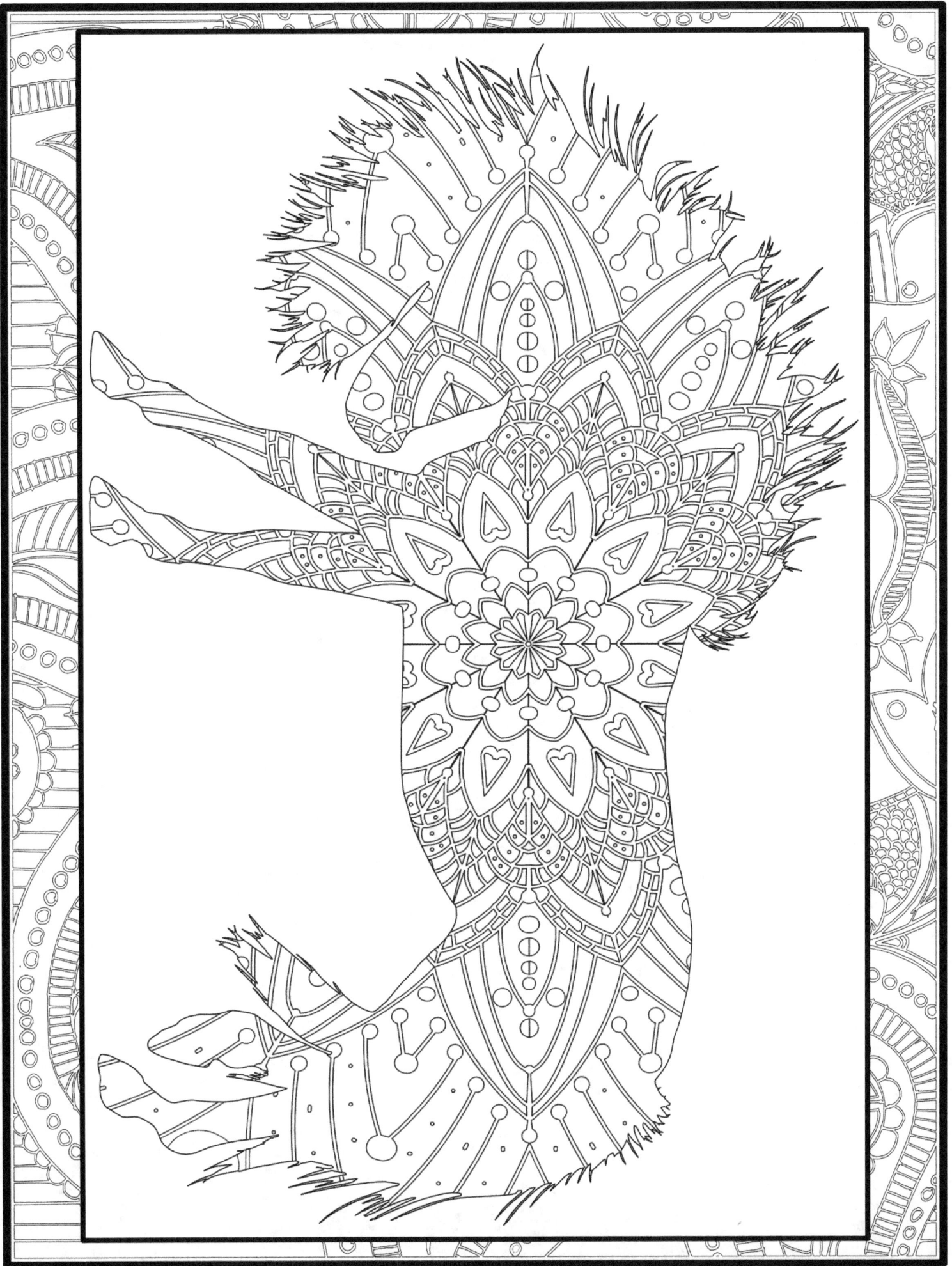

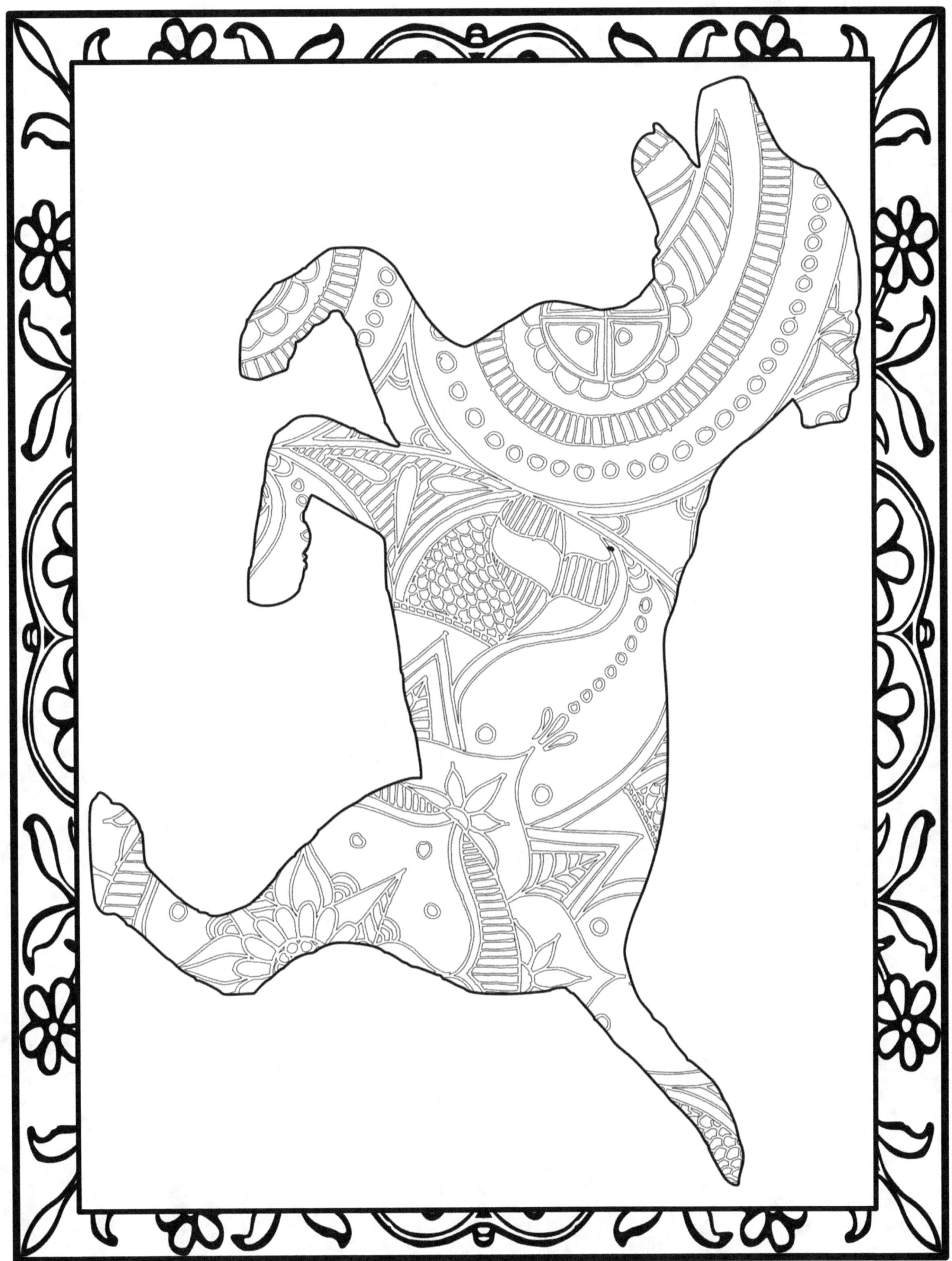

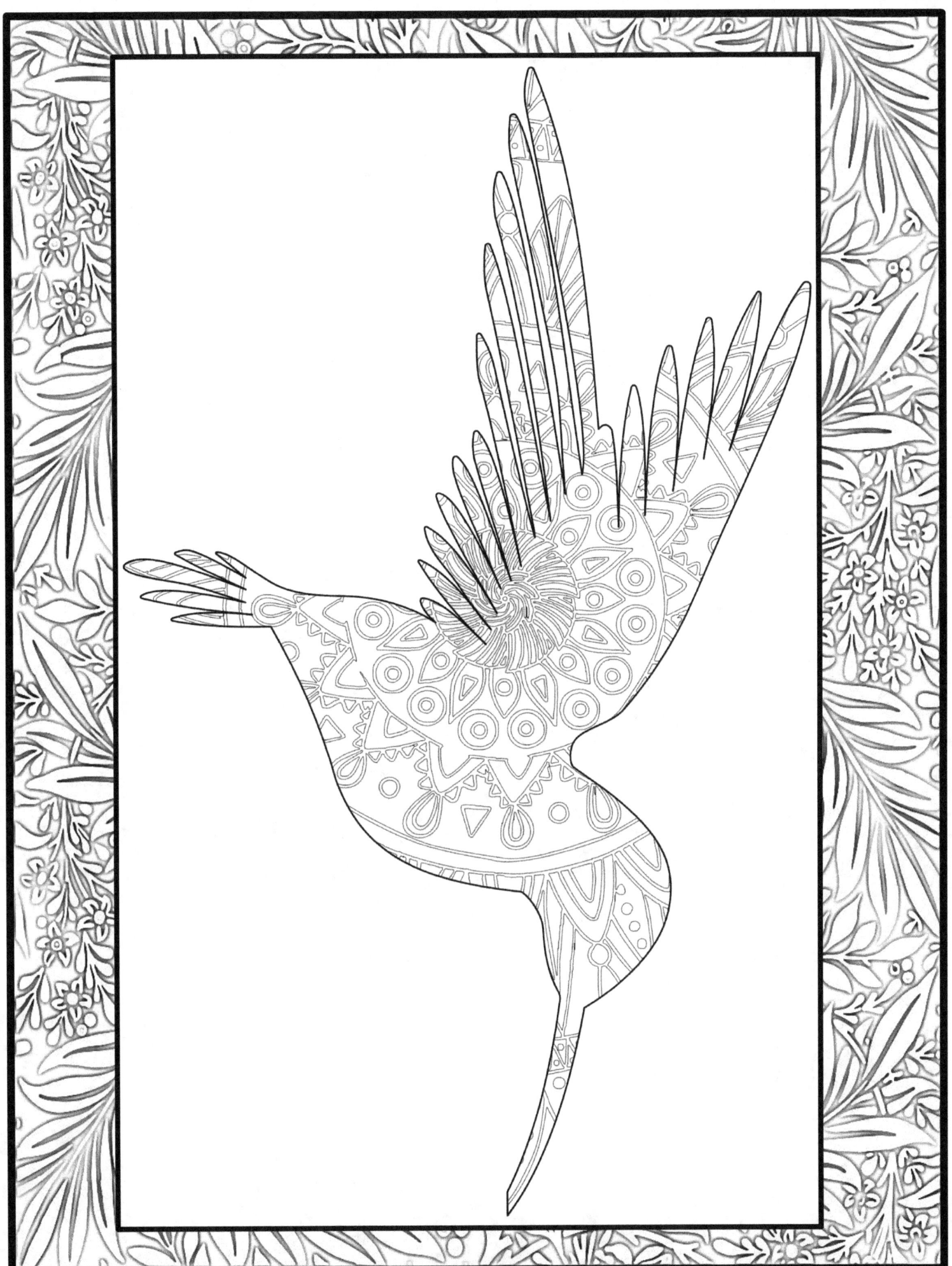

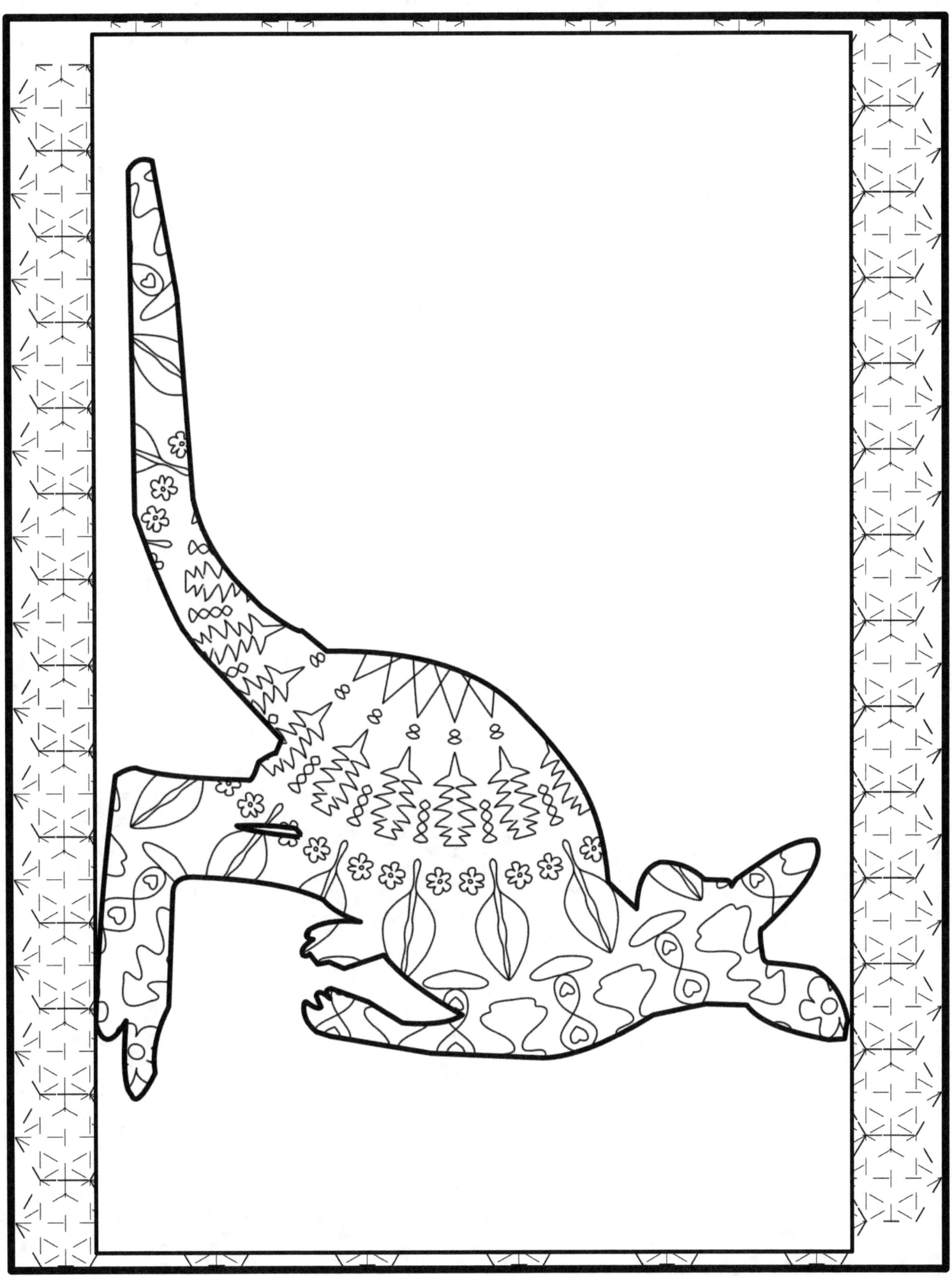

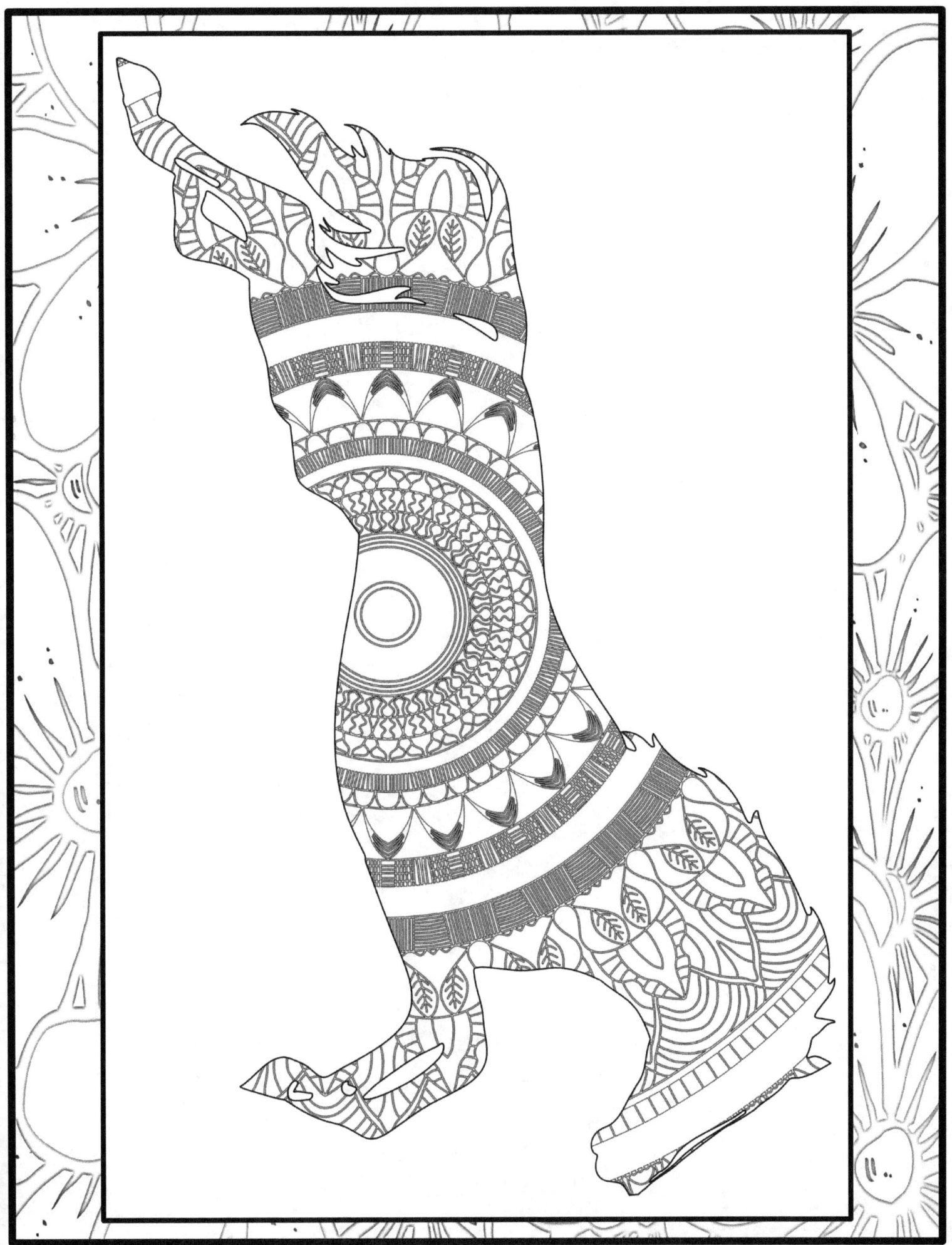

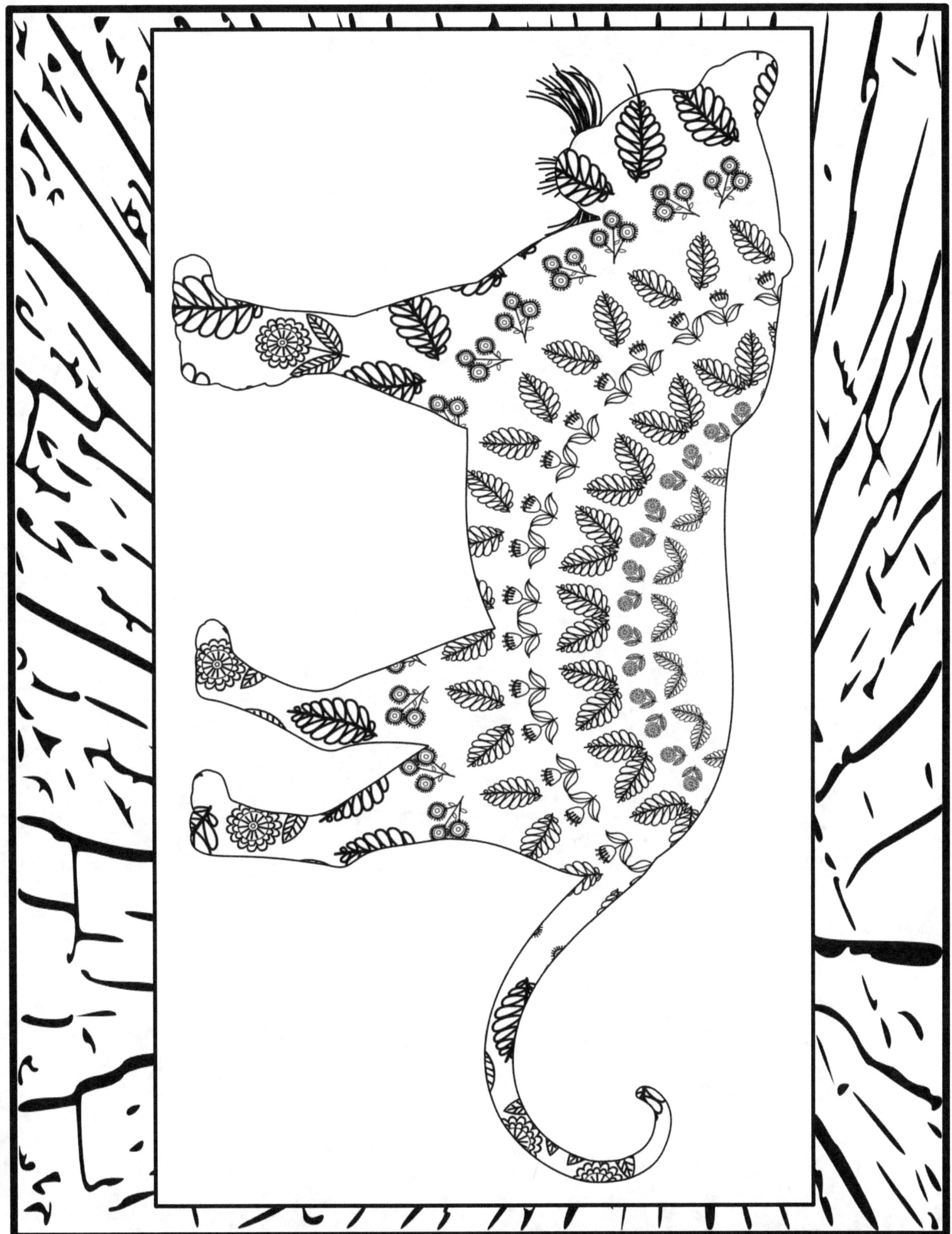

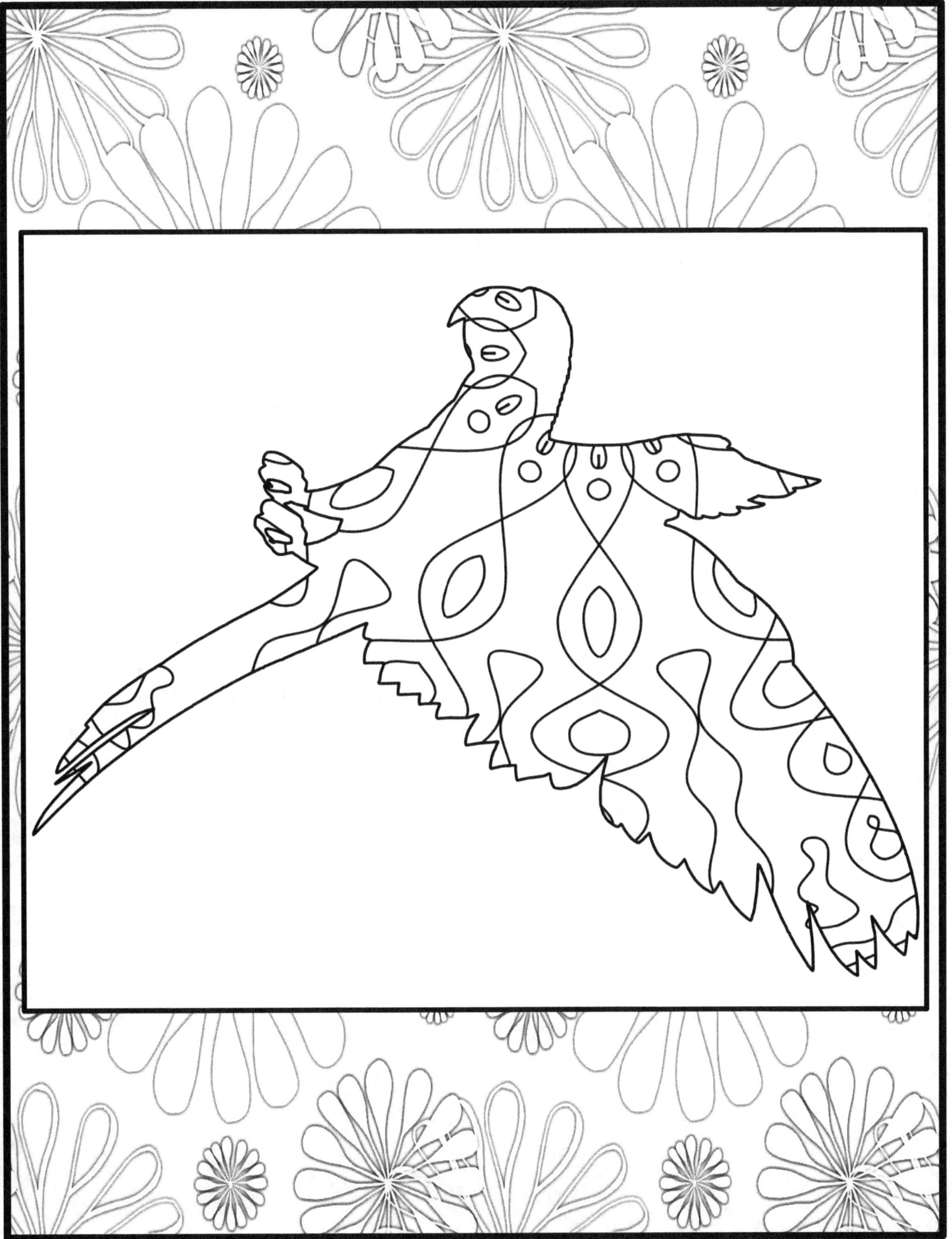

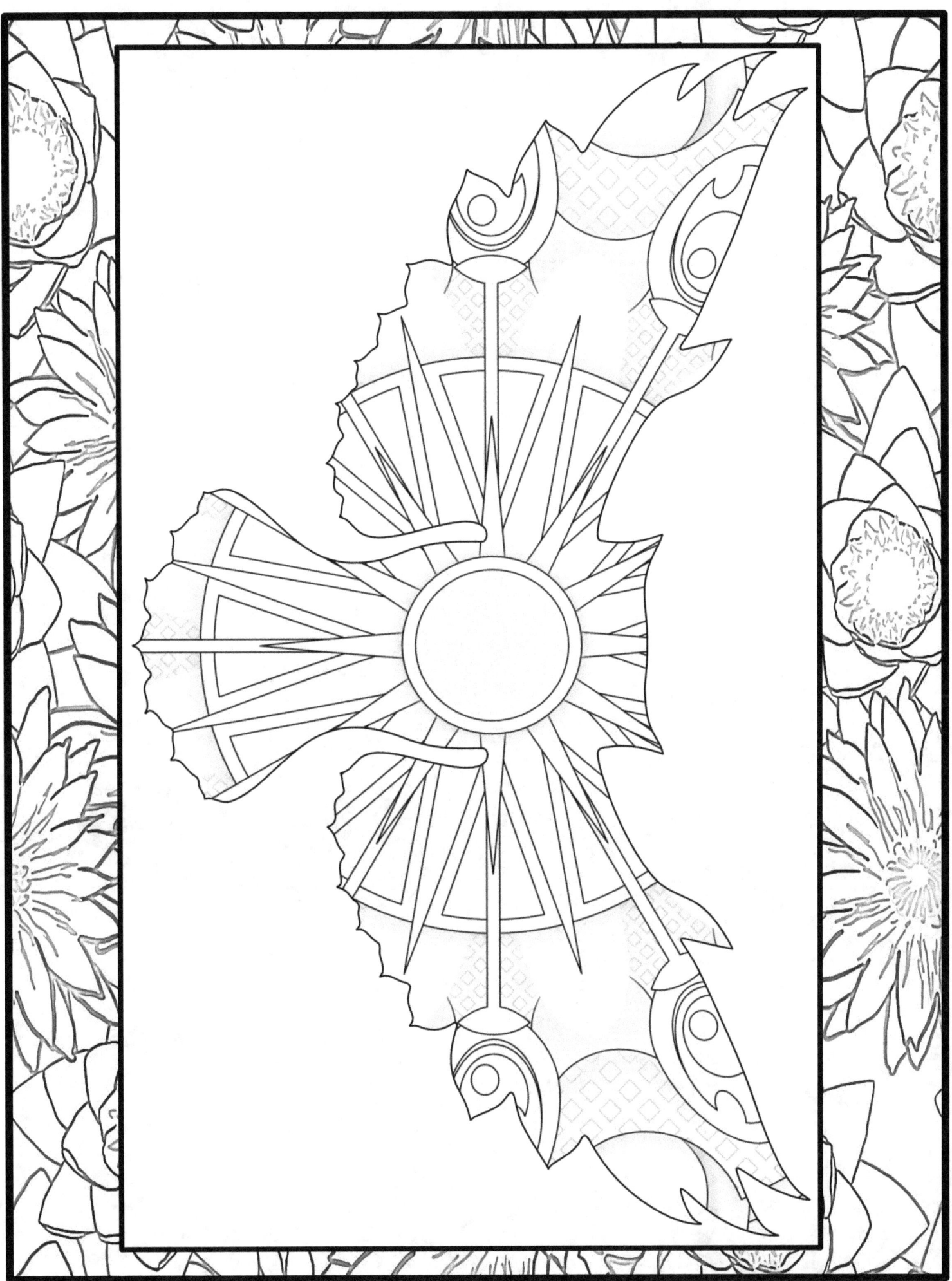

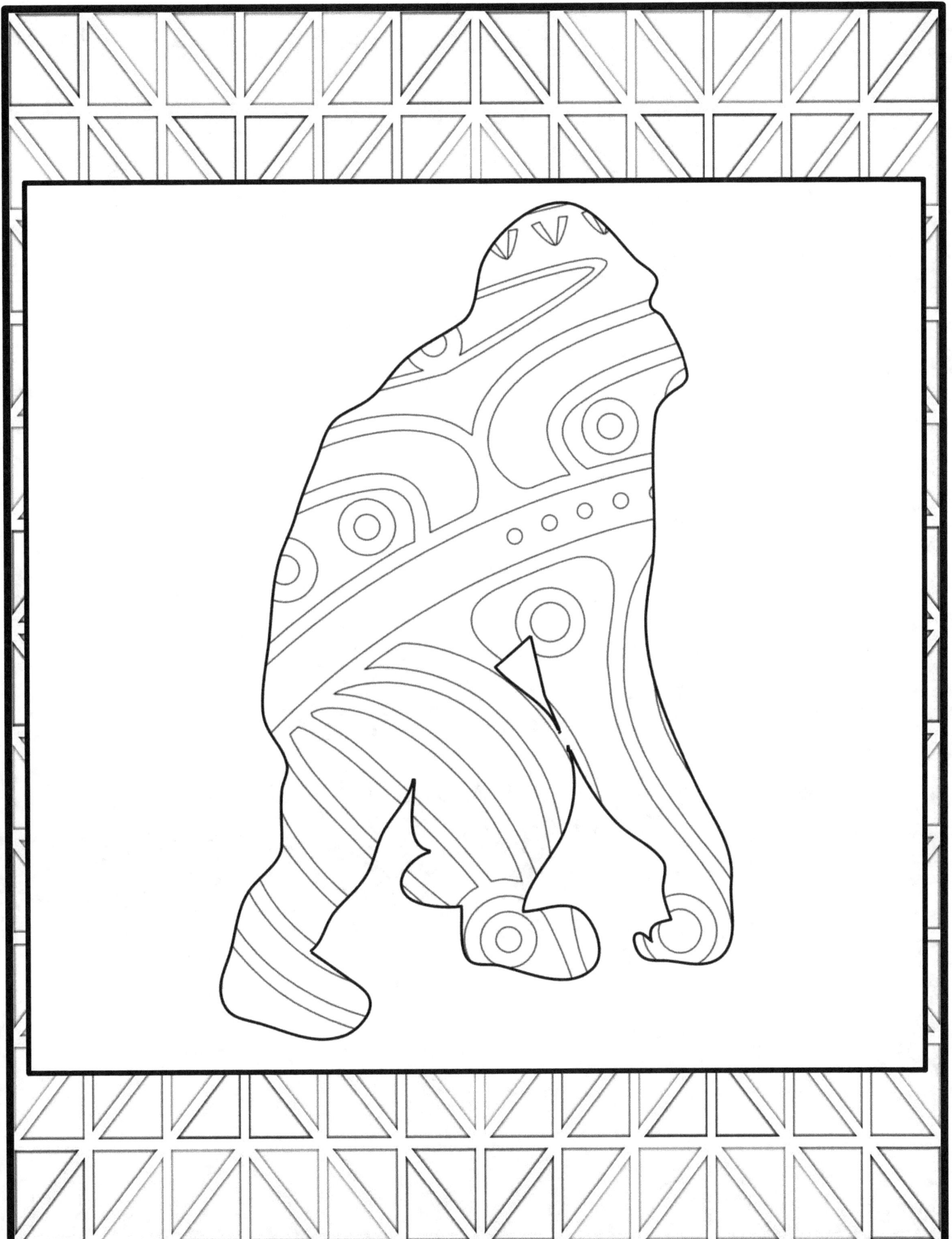

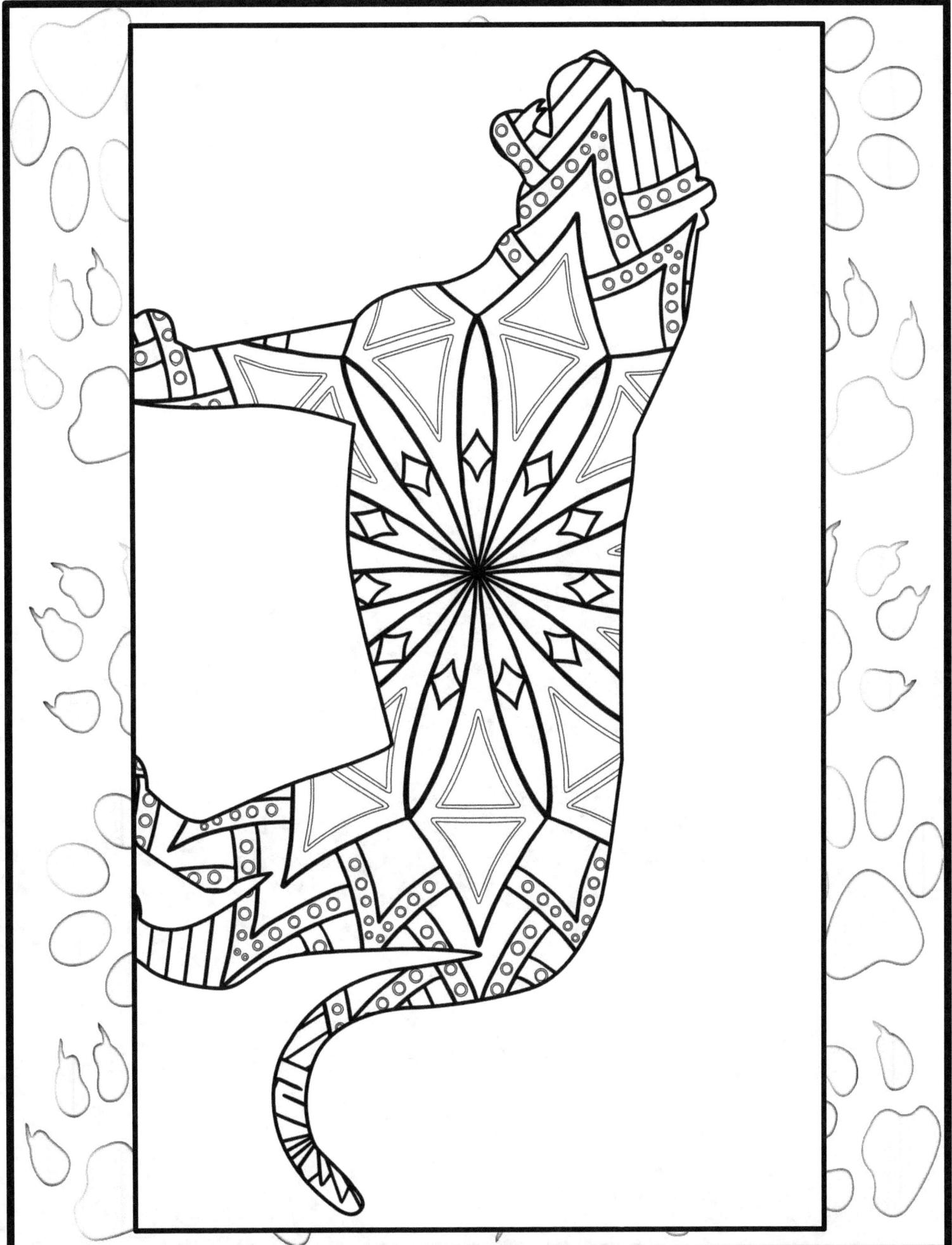

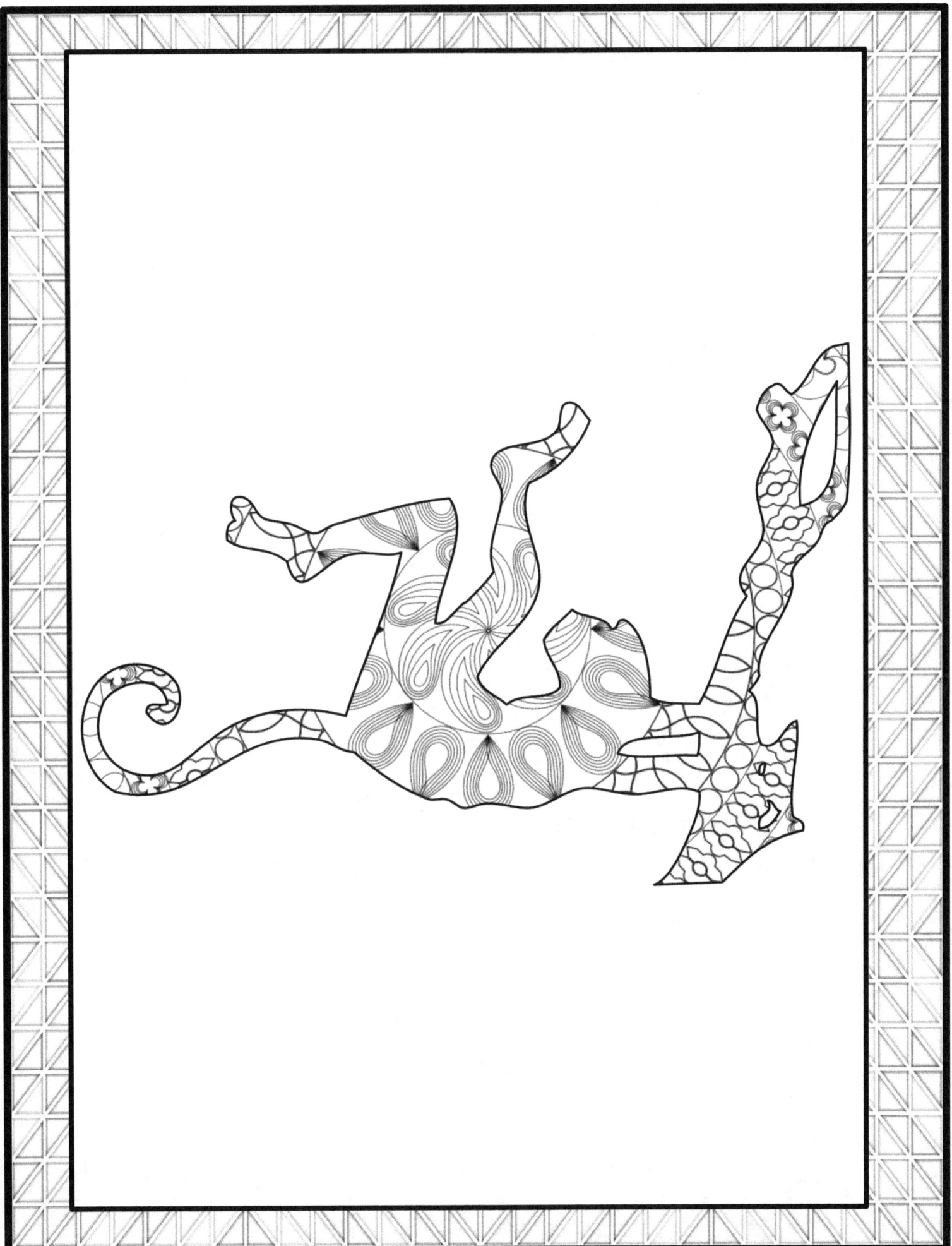

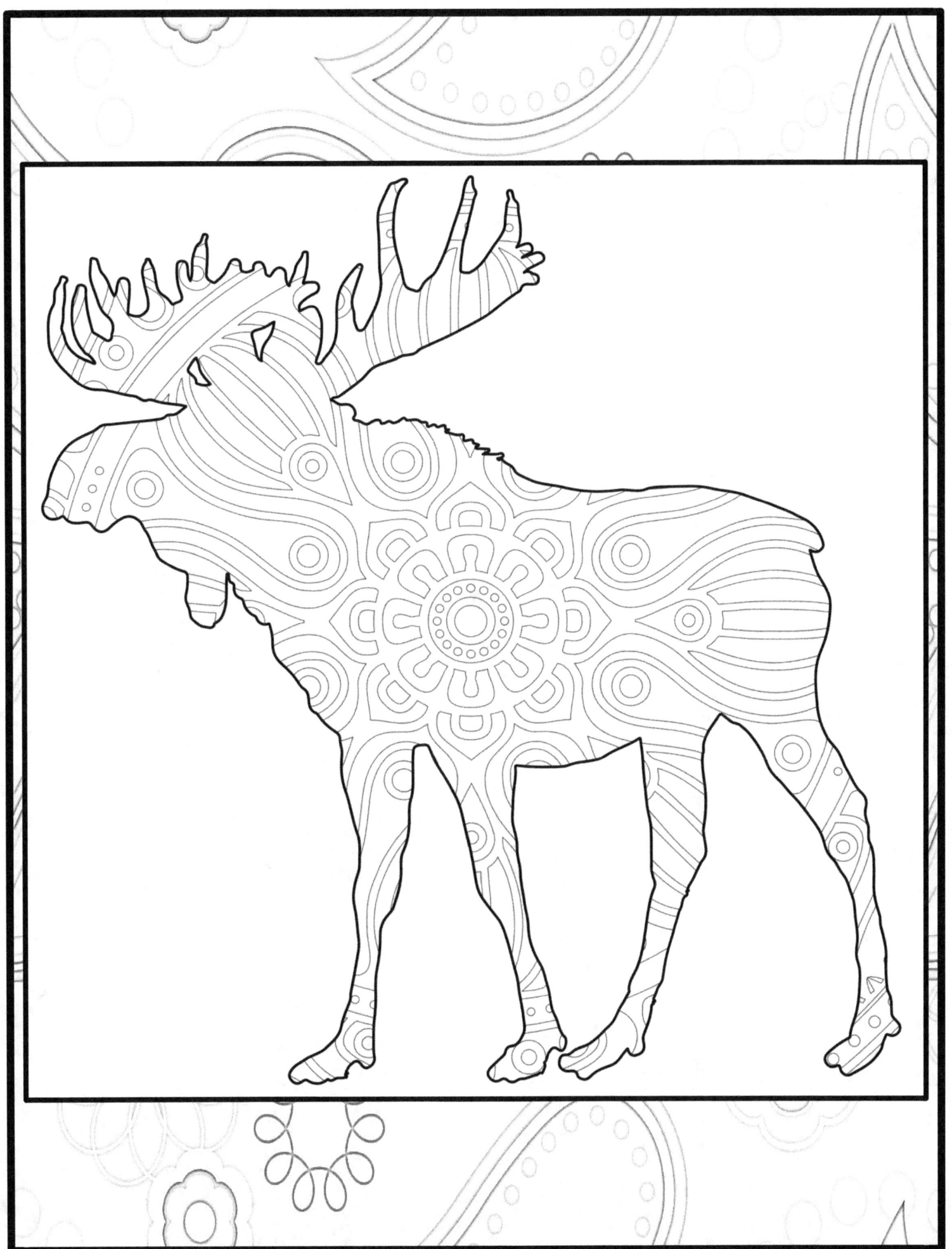

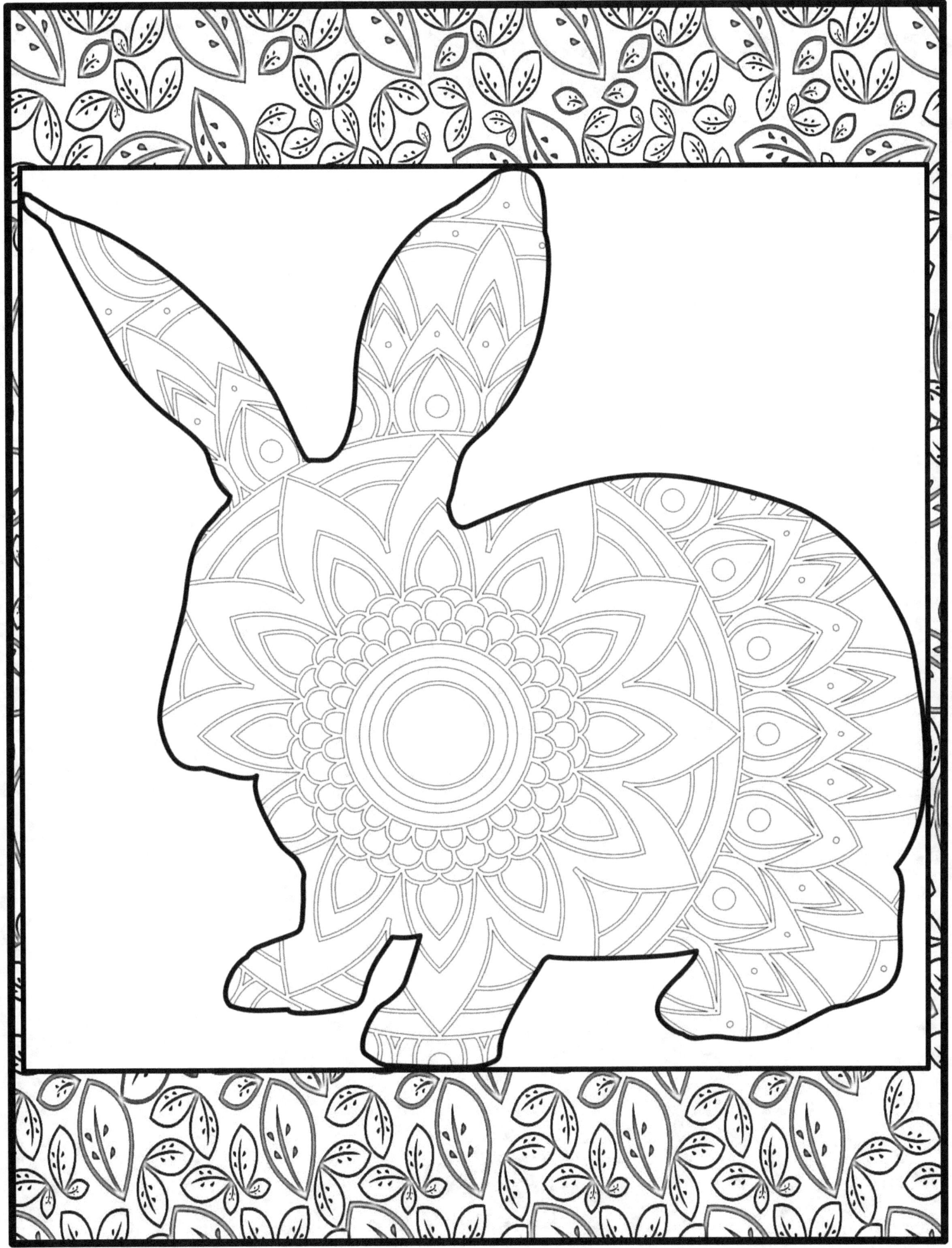

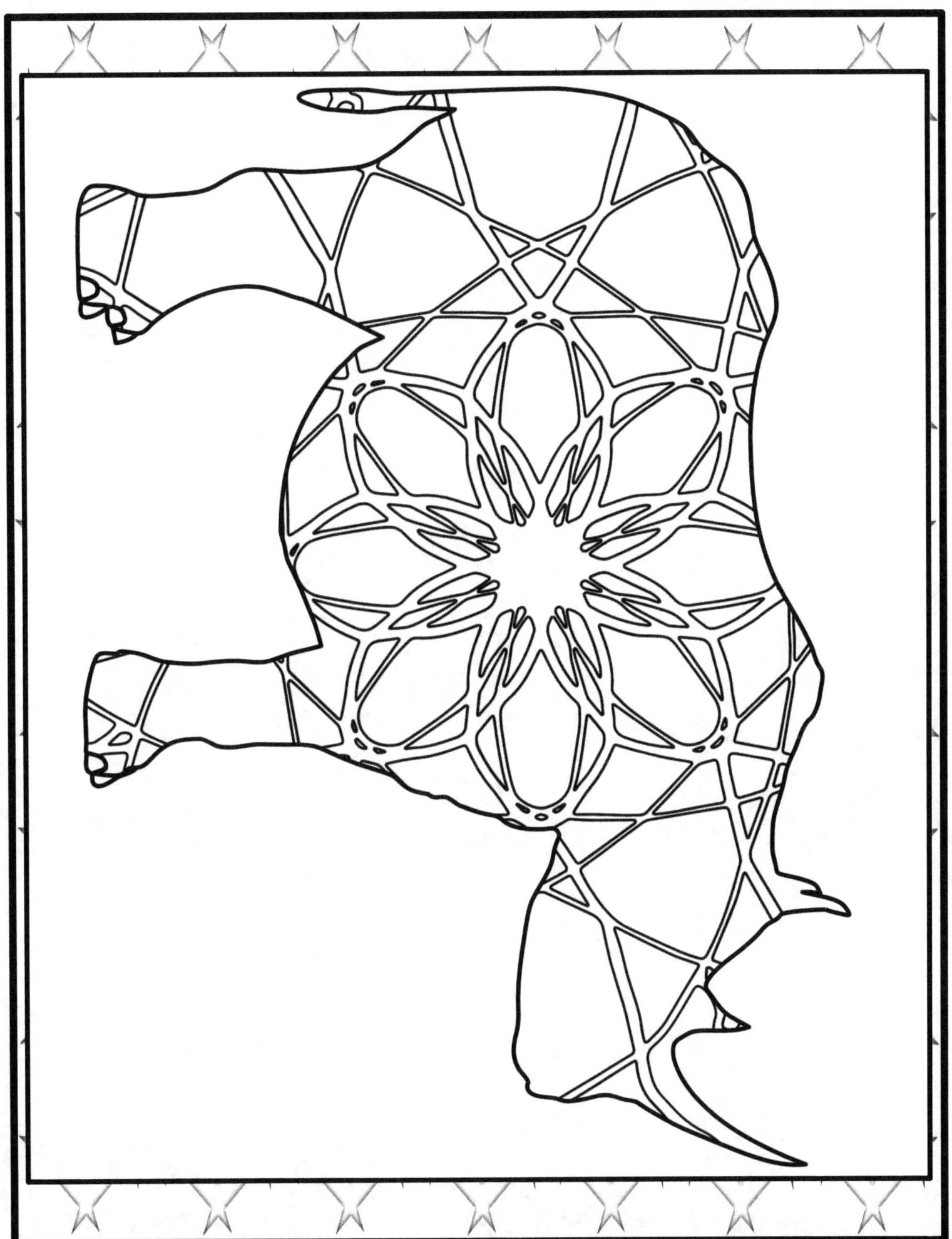

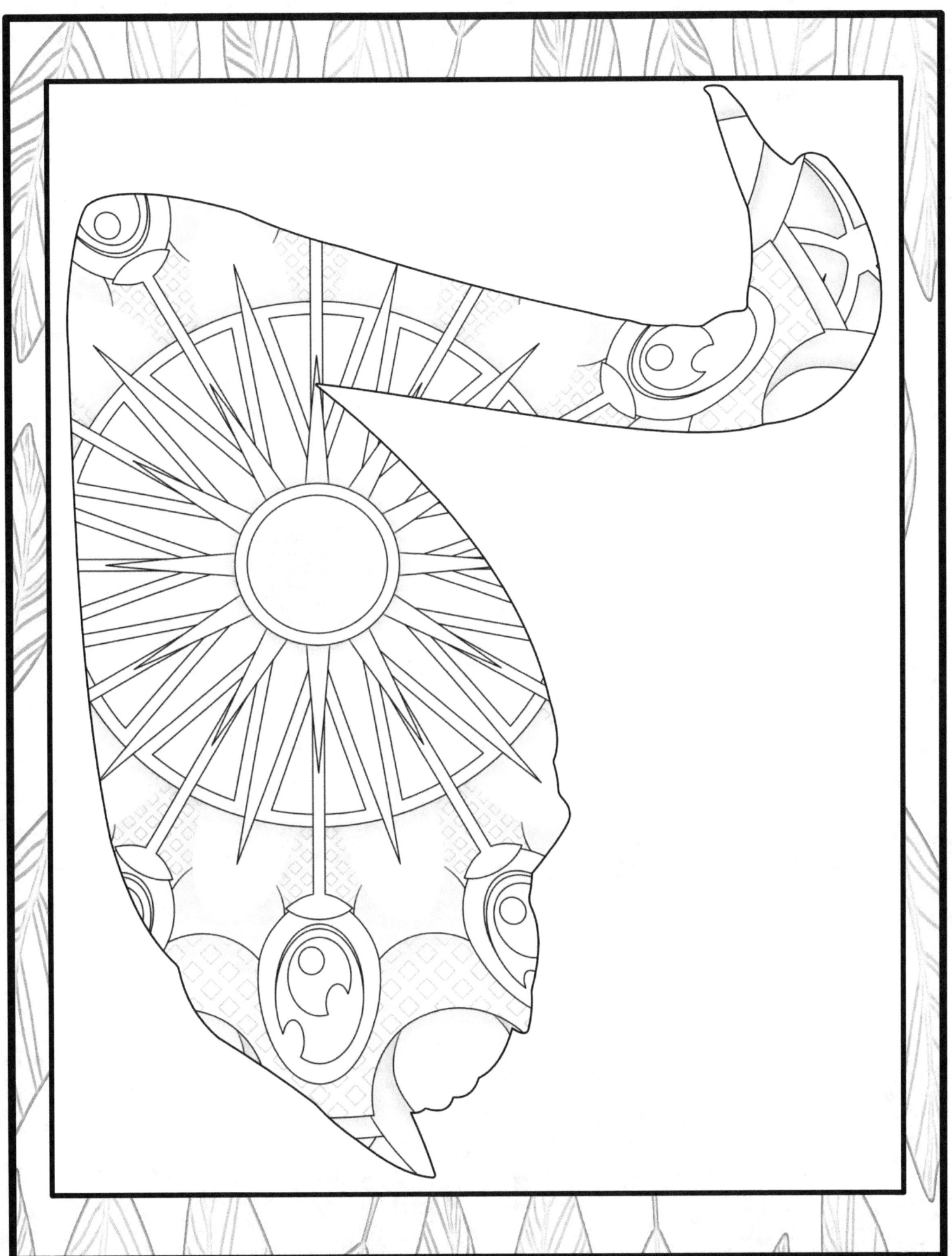

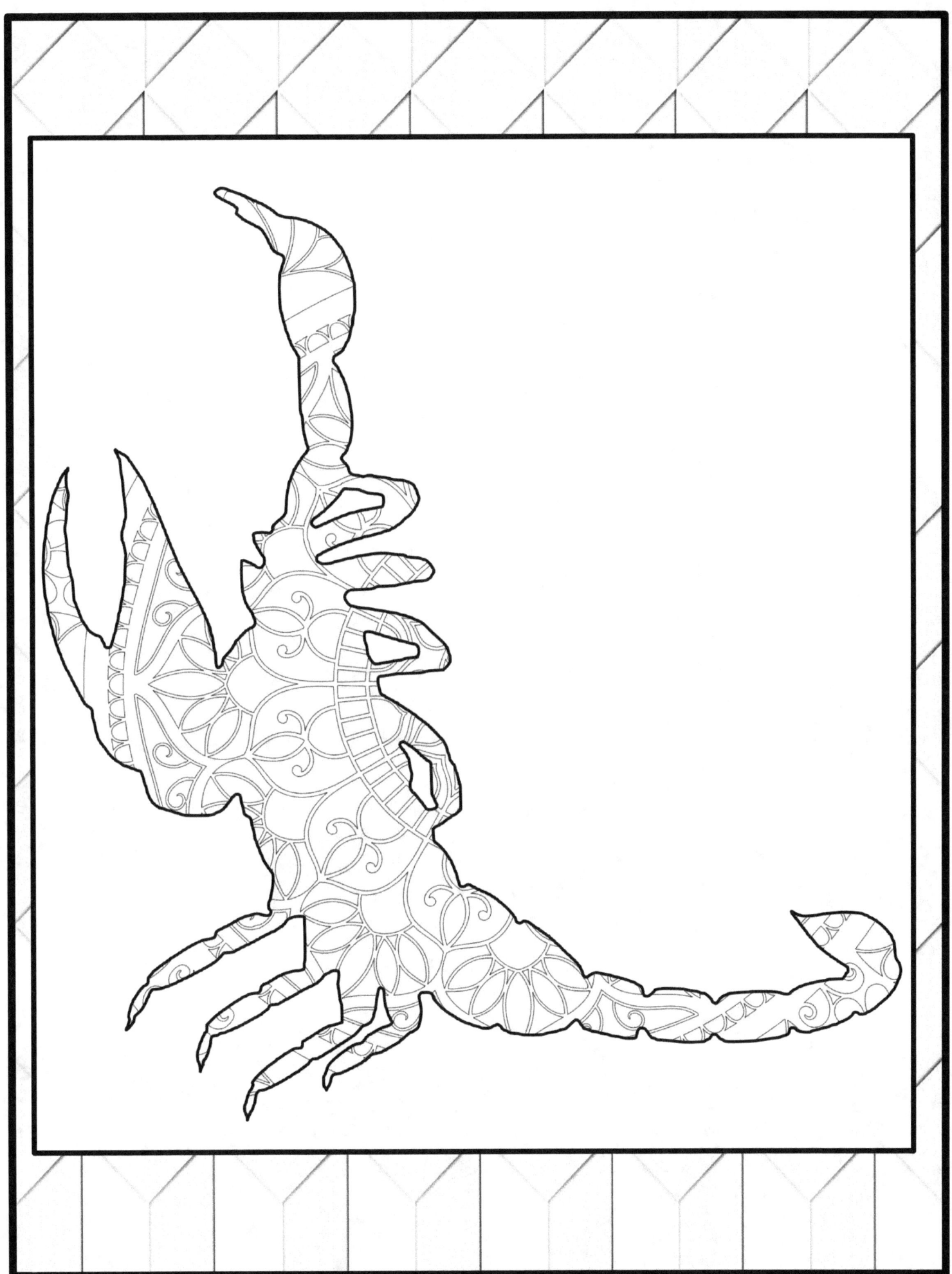

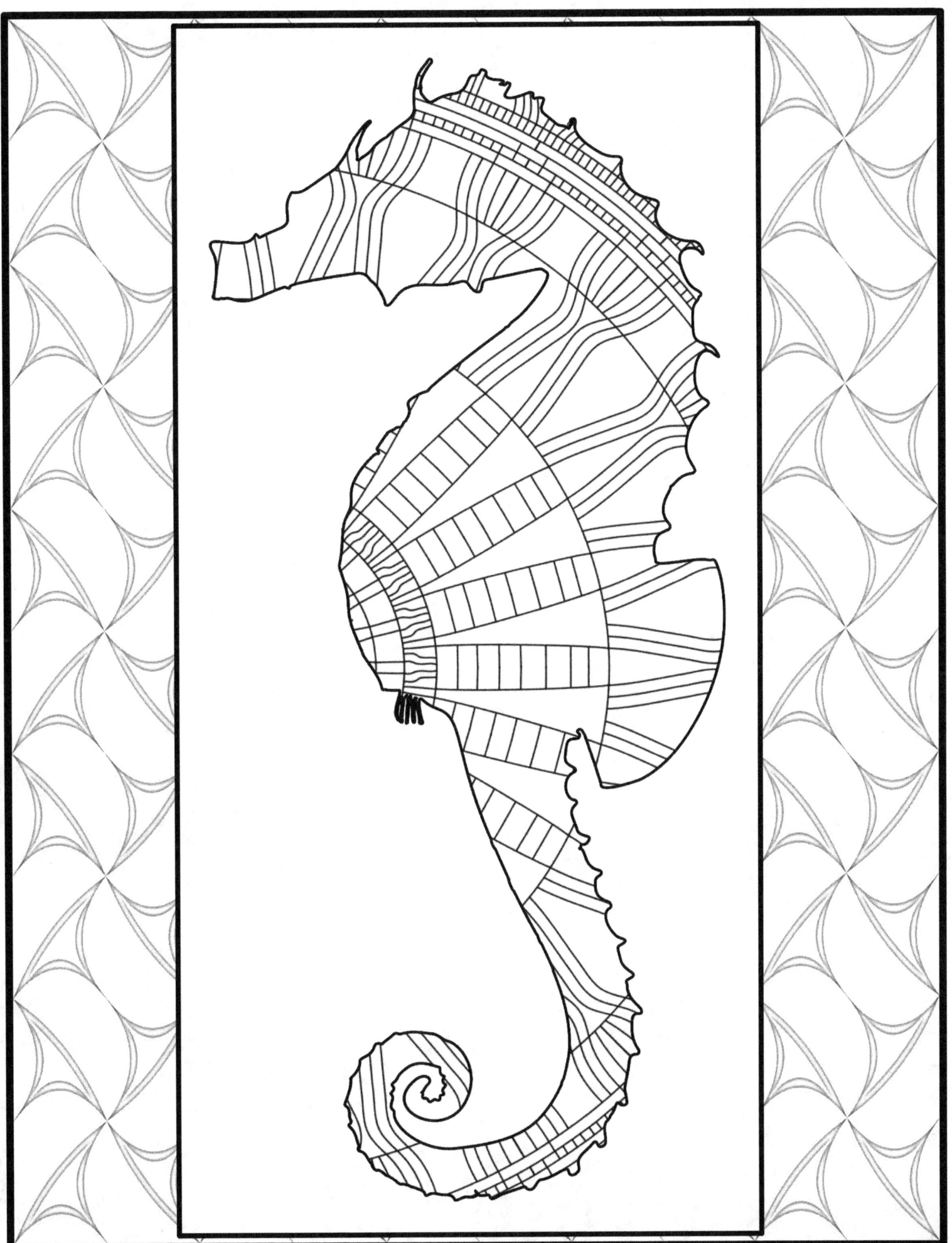

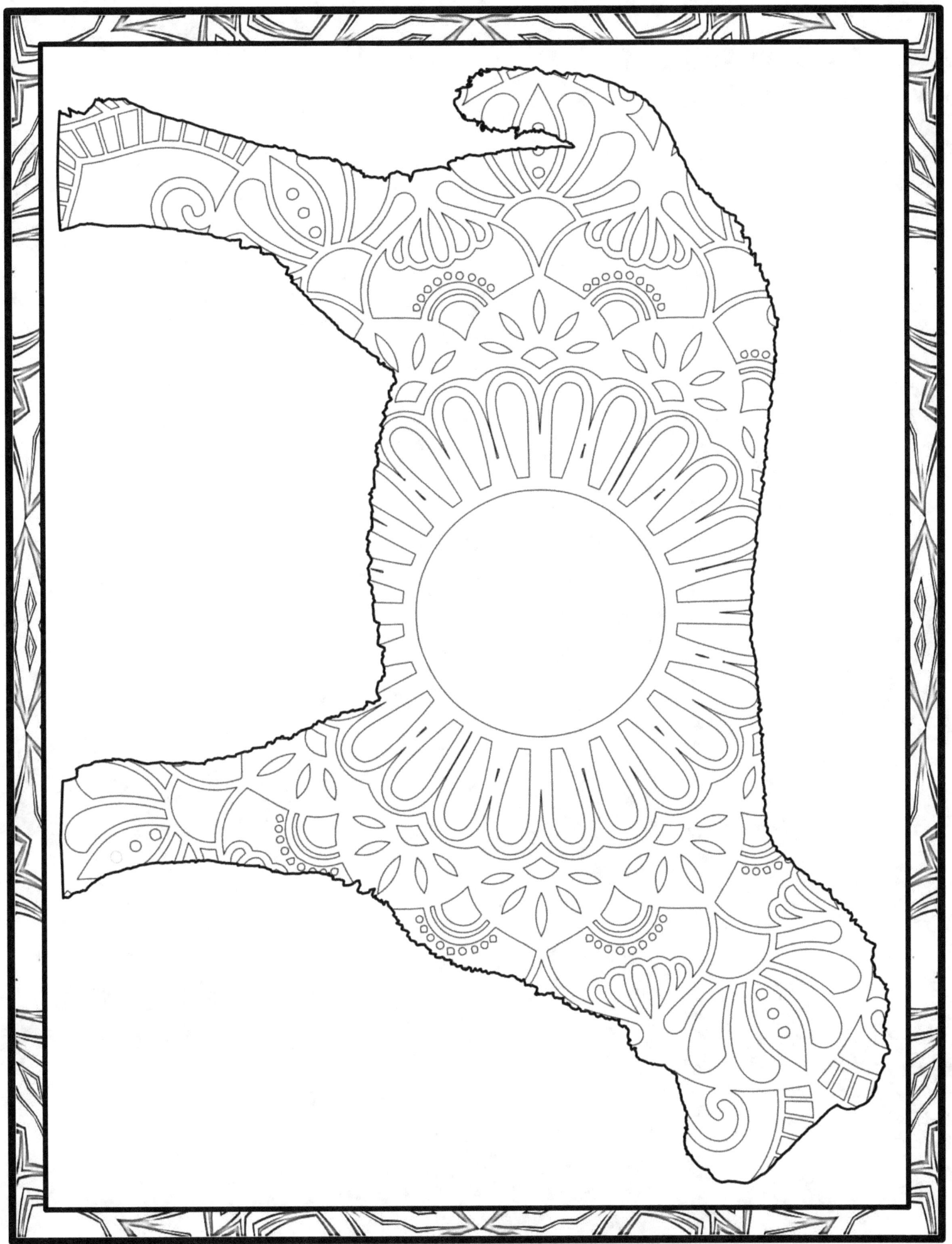

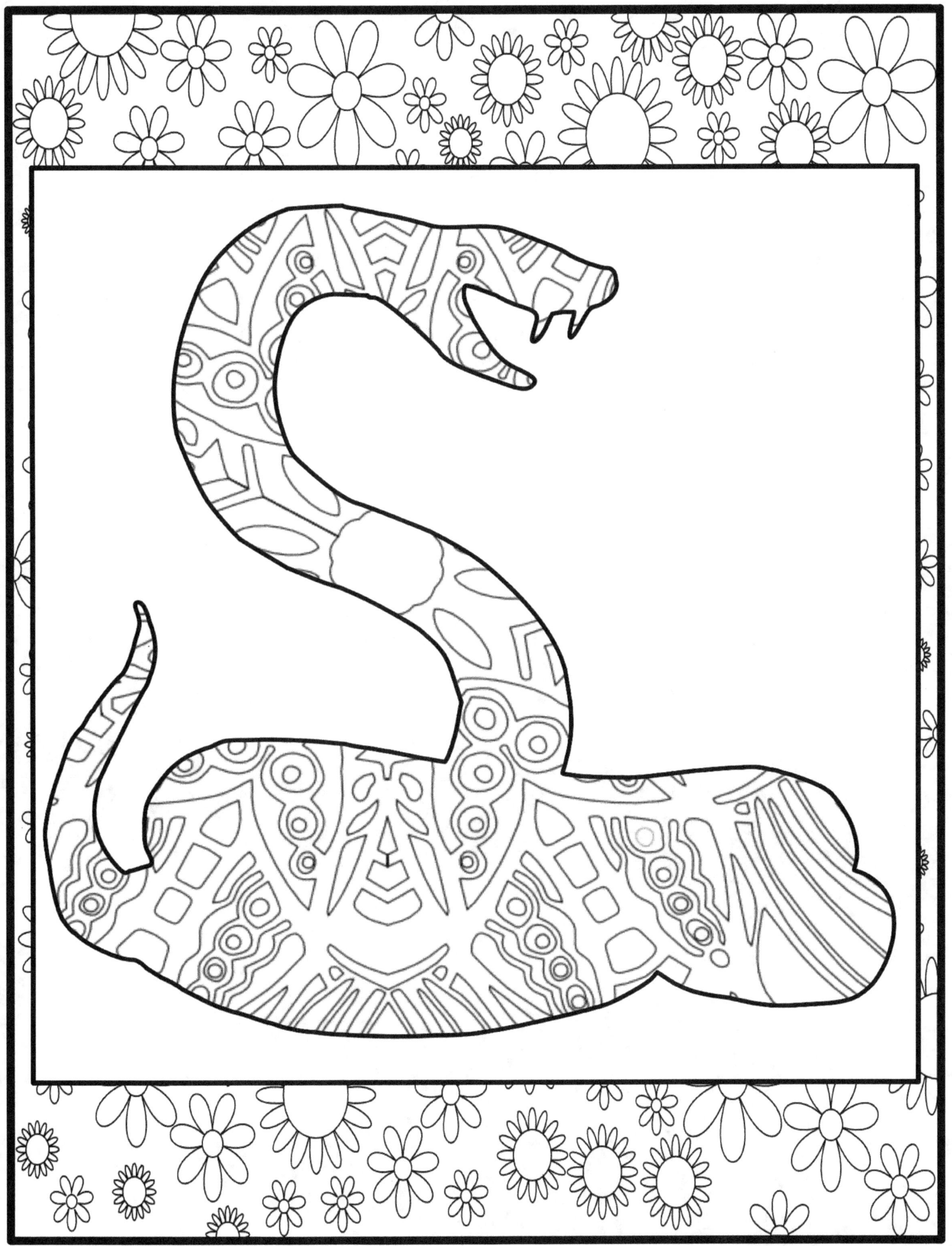

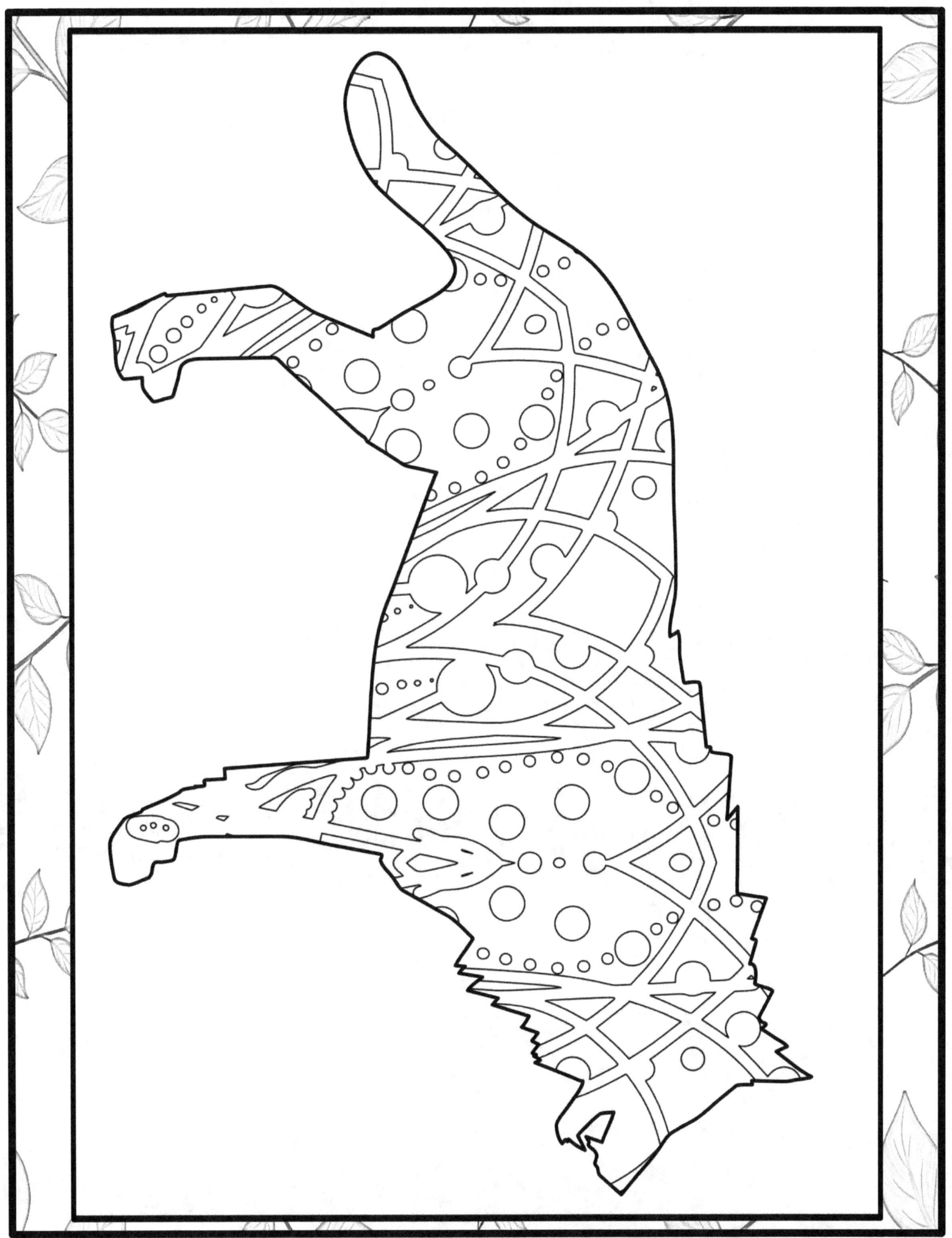

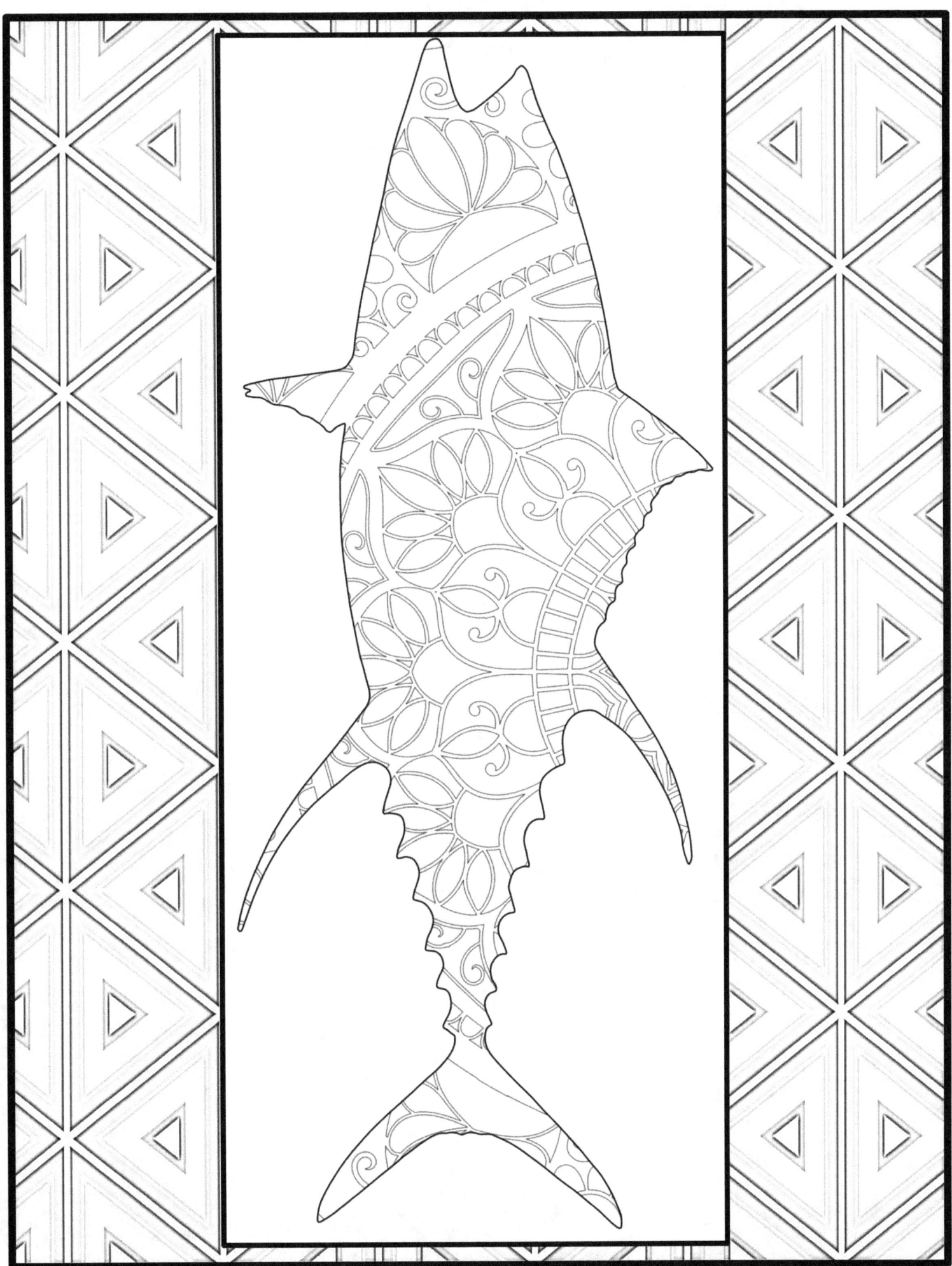

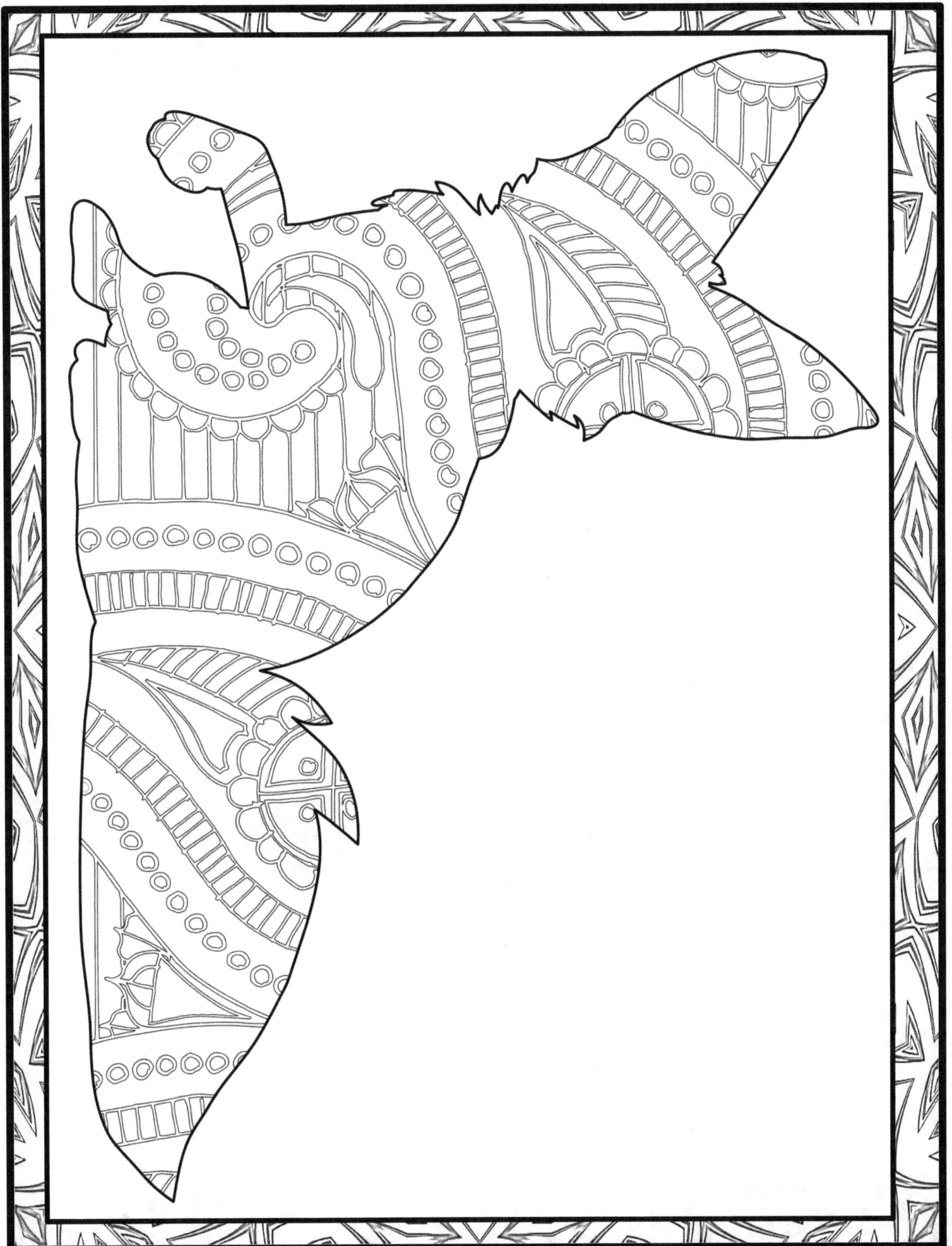